Yukon Re-Run

*A Last Frontier River Trip Repeated by Two Women
Forty-two Years after Their First Run in 1941*

D1601457

Happy Trails !!
Karen Martinsen
Sitka, Alaska
June 3, 1994
Mary Hervin

Yukon Re-Run

A Last Frontier River Trip Repeated by Two Women
Forty-two Years after Their First Run in 1941

By Mary Hervin
and Karen Martinsen

Illustrated by
Dan Thorington

Mary's Road Press

YUKON RE-RUN
By Mary Hervin and Karen Martinsen
Copyright © 1991 by Mary Hervin
First attempt

Library of Congress Catalog Card Number: 91-091934

ISBN: 0-9629288-0-1

Additional copies available at:

> Mary's Road Press
> Box 133
> Gustavus, Alaska 99633

Printed in the U.S.A.

To Phyllis James Kingsbury, partners, and to all of our grandchildren — hers and mine. May they all have some wonderful adventures too.

M.H.

To my best friend Nancy Seamount, and my third grade teacher, Mrs. Arntz, who both encouraged me to write and to believe in my potential.

K.M.

ACKNOWLEDGMENTS

We are grateful for assistance from several people: Mary's family and friends who kept insisting that she write it down; the many wonderful people on the shores of the Yukon River, who seemed sincerely happy to have visitors; Fendal Yerxa for his many helpful suggestions; Mary Lauer who helped us so much with her knowledge of publishing; Sigrid Brudie for editing; and Clothilde, Kathy, Dan, Bob and Janice for their encouragement. Thanks to Paul and Nora Johnson for making the second trip possible and to Hal and Cynthia Lindquist for the many times they helped carry the gear ashore for an old gal. Thanks to Cynthia for her knowledge of plant life. And, of course, thanks to the Macintosh and fax machines, with Karen Martinsen at the helm. With Mary's encouragement, trust, and patience, Karen tied together the many notebooks and scraps of paper scribbled on through all those many years.

M. H.

K. M.

CONTENTS

Re-Run   11

The Lottery of 1941   15

Reflections of a Seasoned Cheechako   27

Trail of the Gold Rush: White Pass and Beyond   37

Grandma's Village   43

Really Living!   53

Birthday Bannock and Church Mug-Up   59

Old Relics   69

River Folks   75

Landscapes   83

Yukon Hospitality   91

Ma Britton   97

The River's Work   101

The Klondike   109

Dawson Revisited   115

Reunion   123

Putting In   129

Roll Up the Sidewalks   135

Bear Country   141

The Lure of the North   149

End Again   159

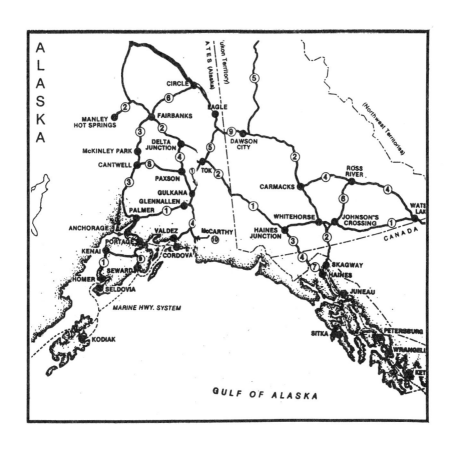

ALASKA

Getting set to cast off again in 1983.

1

Re-Run

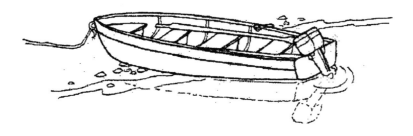

In July, 1983, I was about to retrace a route that I had traveled forty-two years earlier—eight hundred miles down the Yukon River in the Yukon Territory of Canada. In 1941, I traveled the Yukon in a sixteen-foot skiff with my girlfriend Phyllis. I was twenty years old then, and neither Phyl nor I had much experience with boats or rivers. But there was a job waiting for me in Anchorage, and the river was the cheapest and most adventurous way to get to our destination. This time, forty-some years later, I was pursuing it for recreation and to relive grand memories.

My party included old friends Paul and Nora Johnson from Elfin Cove, Alaska, and Hal and Cynthia Lindquist from Tucson, Arizona. I worked on Paul's sportfishing boat the summer before when Hal and Cynthia were visiting Alaska as tourists. The four of us got to talking about the

Yukon River that summer, and before we knew it we had agreed to make the trip down the Yukon the following summer. Of course Paul's wife, Nora, would join us.

I spent the winter planning and daydreaming about re-running the Yukon, and by June I realized that we were really going through with our plans. We would take Paul's eighteen-foot Lund skiff and motor, "putting in" the river at Whitehorse. But Paul and the rest of the group planned to go only as far as Dawson City. That's when I got the idea to call Phyllis and see if she would consider kayaking the rest of the way to Circle City, which was the end of our last voyage.

It seemed natural to end the Yukon trip with Phyllis again. I hadn't had any contact with Phyl for about five years, but over the years we had managed to touch base from time to time. Our lives had taken separate paths, as they always do, but still we had shared great times together. I was sure we could pick up where we left off—in the great outdoors.

I was overjoyed when I called Phyllis to ask if she'd be interested in taking the journey again; she didn't even hesitate, of course she'd do it! I must admit I was a little surprised, especially after all these years, and because I had only given her about six weeks notice! Just like Phyl, though, always willing to go along with anything for an adventure. I would motor down as far as Dawson with my other friends, and Phyllis would fly there to meet me. The two of us would then kayak the remaining 350 miles to Circle City.

The first stage of the trip was a forty-minute flight from Juneau to Skagway in a Cessna 206. Paul and I flew there to meet the rest of the party that was waiting with the car, boats and gear. As we flew above the hanging glaciers that border Lynn Canal, I retraced the route that Phyl and I had taken forty-two years earlier in our little skiff.

"There are dreams... new and old... of paths to be explored... new worlds... new trails untraveled... dim dreams of destiny forever stored with the fabric of life left unraveled."

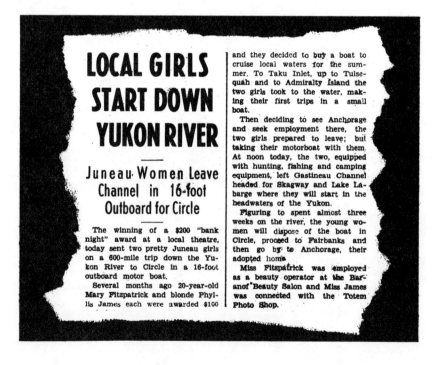

LOCAL GIRLS START DOWN YUKON RIVER

Juneau Women Leave Channel in 16-foot Outboard for Circle

The winning of a $200 "bank night" award at a local theatre, today sent two pretty Juneau girls on a 600-mile trip down the Yukon River to Circle in a 16-foot outboard motor boat.

Several months ago 20-year-old Mary Fitzpatrick and blonde Phyllis James each were awarded $100 and they decided to buy a boat to cruise local waters for the summer. To Taku Inlet, up to Tulsequáh and to Admiralty Island the two girls took to the water, making their first trips in a small boat.

Then deciding to see Anchorage and seek employment there, the two girls prepared to leave; but taking their motorboat with them. At noon today, the two, equipped with hunting, fishing and camping equipment, left Gastineau Channel headed for Skagway and Lake Labarge where they will start in the headwaters of the Yukon.

Figuring to spent almost three weeks on the river, the young women will dispose of the boat in Circle, proceed to Fairbanks and then go by to Anchorage, their adopted home.

Miss Fitzpatrick was employed as a beauty operator at the Baranof Beauty Salon and Miss James was connected with the Totem Photo Shop.

2

The Lottery of 1941

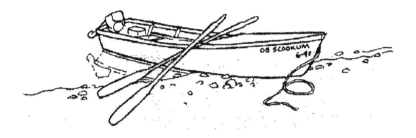

It all started back in Juneau, that striking, lovely coastal capital of Alaska. I had been working in a photographer's shop there for two years. When I had a vacation I went back to my home at Redding, California. But before leaving Juneau, I knew I'd be back. I'd become thoroughly inoculated with the spirit of the northland, and the only thing that bothered me was that I wanted to see more of what lay "up yonder." It was pleasant to see my family and friends again, but somehow the things on the "Outside" that had once appealed to me seemed very dull when I went back on my vacation. My thoughts kept racing back to the high, gleaming snow-capped peaks of Alaska, to the tangy ocean breezes, the jagged glaciers, and all the other wonders of the fabulous North.

I talked constantly about Alaska and what a wonderful place it was. My friend Phyl listened with ever-growing fascination to the tales and experiences I had to relate, and at last she said, "Mary, do you suppose I could find a job up there, too?" With that remark a beautiful friendship and a glorious adventure was born!

After leaving the confusion and hustle of the "lower 48" (as northerners refer to the other states), I returned to my job in Juneau. Phyllis found a job at a beauty parlor. We had a lot of fun; we both liked our jobs and the people we met and worked with.

We managed to buy an old sixteen-foot heavy wooden lapstrake skiff at the beginning of summer, and the two of us spent every spare moment fixing it up. We gave up some of the extras like eating out so that we could pour our meager earnings into our little prize. One night we sawed and hammered until the last minute before dashing up town in order to sign up for a contest at the theater. The drawing wasn't until the following evening and we felt silly wasting such valuable time on a pipe dream. Nonetheless, we ran up there in our paint- and oil-stained slacks and became eligible to win one hundred dollars if one of us won.

Being true working girls our paychecks were quite thoroughly spent long before payday, and buying our little skiff and outboard motor had taken all our savings. One day Phyllis and I made a production out of buying paint for the boat during our lunch hour. Oh yes, to us our skiff was a yacht, and everything had to be purchased under our critical but definitely not nautical eyes! We scarcely knew what "bow and stern" referred to. Neither of us had ever handled an outboard before, and our rowing at first usually managed to shower the other person.

That evening, clad in paint clothes, we set out to paint our boat. When we couldn't find anything to open the paint can with, Phyllis tried prying the lid open with a rusty nail. She was successful, except that when she pushed down, the paint went up! With gray paint from head to foot she said, "Oh well, we didn't want to paint with dull gray anyway. The white will be much prettier."

So a coat of white was brushed on over the nicks and scratches. The truth of the matter was we were in a hurry to paint the "O. B. Scookum" before too many people saw how old it really was. OB was the official registration for boats with outboard motors. (Today the Coast Guard uses the initials MV and FV for motor or fishing vessels.) Skookum is a Pacific Northwestern word meaning tough and strong. We had never seen the word spelled, but we liked it, so we went with what looked right. While Coast Guard men watched from their boat and laughed at us, we finished up the job. About midnight we headed for home carrying some lumber that we planned to get cut uptown.

Soon a friend came running up to us and after stammering for a few seconds tried to tell us that we had *each* won $100 at the theater! Of course we never believed her. That was nearly impossible, but I'll admit we were both plenty excited and grabbed each other and ran toward town. We were too excited to realize that even more outrageous was the fact that we had registered at the theater nearly two years apart from each other. We had gone together to get the fifty-cent ticket that activated our registration. It was more than unlikely that both of our names would be drawn on the same night. By the time we were in the center of town everyone was congratulating us on our unbelievable luck, although they would never know that $200 could mean so much to anyone.

The next morning I dashed down to Juneau Cold Storage where my brother Larry was selling fish. I jumped across the slippery dock and around the halibut waiting to be deheaded and frozen. "Phyllis and I each won a hundred dollars at the theater last night!" I shouted to Larry. Now, Larry is one of the best Irish storytellers you'll ever meet, so he was almost disgusted. His first remark was, "My gosh, Mary, if you're going to tell a story, tell it so someone will believe you." So I invited him to have lunch with me. By lunchtime I had gotten the two checks from the theater manager, who knew that Phyllis and I were roommates. He too could hardly believe that the two of us had each won.

Most of the money went toward the boat and the many weekend trips we enjoyed. Our friends lectured and warned us about believing we could rely on such luck all the time. I do think, though, that luck must have been the third passenger on the O. B. Scookum when I look back on some of the adventures we survived.

On one trip to Turner Lake, in Taku Inlet, we got the wild notion to run the Yukon River. My job was ending in several weeks, but the same company had a position for me in Anchorage. Back then, there was no such thing as relocation costs, and we certainly couldn't afford to ride the expensive Alaskan steamship that could take us as far as Seward. From there we would have to take a train to Anchorage. As we thought about it, the Yukon seemed like the way to go. Even before this idea dawned on us, we had spent a lot of our free time poring over maps, studying Interior Alaska and the Yukon, making plans for the day when we might set sail for the romantic land of the golden Klondike. Never did we think the opportunity would come so soon. In a matter of weeks, Phyllis and I would be on our way!

We read everything we could find about the Interior— stories of the gold rush to the Klondike, all about the fabulous days of '98. We were all ears, willing and eager to absorb every story anyone was willing to tell us. Gullible to the nth degree, we believed everything we heard. We have since learned not to be so naive; some of the yarns were pretty tall! As a matter of fact, we can tell some pretty tall ones ourselves, now!

The Alaska summer was already on the wane, and signs of fall were in the air when, on September 4, 1941, we loaded our skiff with supplies, sleeping bags, tarp, and the usual camping equipment. We then cranked up the small outboard motor and headed up the channel toward Skagway.

Friends waved us off and threw wreaths of wildflower blossoms overboard as we headed out for Skagway, the gateway of the '98 gold rush, eighty miles north of Juneau. The trip up Lynn Canal took us nearly a week because we were often rowing or working on the outboard motor.

The first evening out of Juneau found us camped in one of our favorite spots above Eagle River. A strong southeaster had come up, assuming gale-like proportions. We didn't want to take any chances so early in our voyage. From huge driftwood logs we built a roaring campfire and felt quite snug despite the fact that most of our time was spent dodging the smoke, which billowed and swirled around in every direction. We had been told that a stump standing beside a campfire would serve as a chimney. Game to try anything once, we set up the stump; but it wasn't long before our makeshift chimney burned out at the base and fell with a crash into the blazing fire. We still had smoke.

After a hearty dinner we watched the sun set gloriously over Sentinel Island. Sitting there sipping our hot tea, we pondered the long trip we were tackling. Thanks to the advice of our many friends, not a few of whom were skeptical about our making such a journey, both Phyl and I had enough advice and pointers stored up in our heads to get us clear around the world! How many of those would turn out like the chimney?

Beside the glowing campfire we unrolled our sleeping bags and turned in for the night, scarcely able to sleep for the excitement of being on our way at last! At about one-thirty, we had to move to the shelter afforded by a thick cluster of trees to get out of the rain.

At five-thirty we were up and shoving our boat into the quickly receding tide. The boat was heavy, and the rocks were slippery—and before long we each had taken an unexpected morning dip. It looked, then, as if our troubles were really starting, for we discovered a wide split in the bottom of our faithful Scookum. Luckily, we found an old apple box on the beach and managed to patch the hole, sealing it with wax from a few bottles of jelly which we had packed with our grub.

Again the wind came up sharply, and, although we knew better, we pushed off. Everything went well as long as we quartered each wave. At about noon we reached Berner's Bay. As it was far too rough to attempt a crossing at the mouth of the bay, we decided to follow the shore and see what it looked like. We were just inside the bay when the motor quit—something we'd hoped wouldn't happen to us. And, as is usually the case with outboard motors, ours quit for no good reason that we could see. Torrents of rain started pouring down. A short distance up the beach we spotted a deserted ranch house and raced to its shelter.

No two girls ever worked harder on anything they knew so little about than we did on that wretched motor! We worked on it all the rest of that day, taking it apart and putting it together again after adjusting this or that. When we thought it was okay, we'd try to start it; but our only reward was a few feeble "put-puts." We decided to return to the motor the next day.

We took a walk along a moss-padded trail in the dense trees and found a spring bubbling up from under a tall spruce. This enchanting scene cheered us up considerably. After some lunch, we took a brisk hike along the sandy beach of a well-protected cove. We brought our rifle along and took a few practice shots at the bracket fungi that grew on the trees. From that display of skill, we decided it was just as well we didn't have to depend upon our luck or shooting ability for food along our journey!

The next morning we were up with the dawn and breakfasted on hot cakes, bacon, and steaming coffee. A rancher who lived in a cabin nearby came down to the beach to investigate our fire. He pitched in like a good scout and helped us with our stubborn motor; and, after a few hours, the O. B. Scookum, apparently all right, was again under way.

The outboard sputtered along indifferently for another twenty miles, then gave up the ghost and died. By that time our tempers were mounting by leaps and bounds. We began to row, saying things about that motor that weren't flattering in the least. It was hard going against the strong outgoing tide of Lynn Canal, so, after two hours of straining and puffing,

Phyl decided to try the motor just once more. It ran like a charm after the first crank! If you've ever owned one of those pestiferous contraptions, you probably know just how temperamental they can be!

It was Saturday night, and we camped at Battery Point. Dead tired, we rolled into our sleeping bags. Even a crackling in the brush didn't bother us as something came down the hillside. Sleep is a wonderful protector!

The following day was really one to give the acid test to novice voyagers! We had high hopes of reaching Skagway; but after several minutes during which the motor ran beautifully, it was suddenly drowned by an on-rushing wave. It got such a thorough soaking that all the cranking in the world wouldn't make it budge.

By then the wind was too strong for the makeshift sail we erected while splashing around in the so-called Lovers' Lane of the Seven Seas. We took the sail down and scanned the almost perpendicular rock walls for a place to land. There was no alternative; my still-inept rowing was no match for the strength of that sea. All too quickly we found ourselves between those uninviting rock walls in a crevice about ten feet wide. Our supplies were drenched and we even feared losing our boat.

By dint of much effort we soon had all our supplies and equipment on the top of a rock bluff where thick trees offered some measure of protection. We were both wet from head to foot. That didn't bother us much, but the scraping of the

Scookum against the rocks was almost more than we could bear.

At last I suggested to Phyl that we should sink the boat, for, by resting on the bottom, it seemed she wouldn't be broken to bits. Phyl was aghast and asked where I'd ever heard of such a silly idea, and I replied that I hadn't, but that I had heard of lots of boats breaking up against the rocks. So, testing the anchor line, we tipped the boat sidewise; but, to our surprise, we found we couldn't sink it! That was some consolation.

We built a fire, made camp, and draped our clothes from the overhanging spruce limbs to dry. Everything was soaked, but with all that water around us, we found there wasn't a drop to drink! We found a spot with some seepage and dug down a couple feet, managing to get enough water for a pot of coffee. To be on the safe side, we boiled it hard, only to spill it all before the coffee grounds settled. It just went to show, as Phyl philosophically observed, that the water wasn't fit to drink. In our hurry to get under way that morning, we had left the can opener behind. But we managed to open tinned provisions with a hatchet, which was rather messy if the first whack wasn't right where it was intended to land.

We made a windbreak from the shore with the tarp, and the natural covering overhead helped ward off the drenching rain. Soon we were snug and cozy, lolling in our sleeping bags and laughing about the events of the day. It just wasn't "our time," we decided, or we never could have lived through them.

Much to our disgust we found another split in our boat the next morning and had to add another patch to the already fancy patchwork design. The water was still too rough for rowing the heavily laden boat around the point which projected about a hundred yards out into the water, so we each took an oar and rowed the Scookum empty for a quarter of a mile. Then we portaged our supplies over the hill and by nine-thirty were off, determined to reach Skagway or bust! Wind and tide were with us, each wave hitting the O. B. Scookum squarely on the stern and literally pushing us forward. With both of us rowing we made the last sixteen miles in less than four hours.

Along our course the waterfalls seemed to crash straight down from the tops of the peaks. Most of these streams formed from glaciers atop the mountains, and the smoky blue veils of water falling into the sea presented a breathtaking spectacle. We were both busy rowing and bailing, but sights of that sort couldn't be overlooked. Neither of us wasted much time talking, and for the first time in our lives, we even forgot about food!

Along the way we passed porpoises that were leaping and springing at each other in what appeared to be a race to the finish. They were not more than fifty yards from our boat, and our hearts were in our mouths as those graceful creatures dove and shot past us. [I have learned a lot about marine life since 1941 and realize now what a grand pastime it is for porpoises to play off the bows of boats. They will leap across each other to catch the current streaming along the hull of a boat, and sometimes they will even strike the hull as they glide through the water.]

3

Reflections of a Seasoned Cheechako

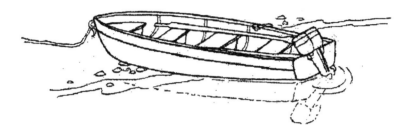

It was a beautiful summer day in 1983 as Paul and I flew above Lynn Canal. How nice to be sitting in the comfort of a plane, warm and dry, while the pilot took care of any worries! I recalled the many predicaments of that first voyage up Lynn Canal, some a little scary and some hilarious. The journey from Juneau to Skagway had taken about six days of hard labor and resulted in a thinning about the waistline. Now, as I snacked on a Baby Ruth candy bar, the trip took about forty-five relaxing minutes. I had to remind myself how a little bit of money and a few modern conveniences make things faster and more accessible. But I wondered if such ease had taken a bit of the risk and exhilaration out of life. By the time we landed at Skagway I was excited about new adventures and couldn't wait to be off for Whitehorse.

In 1941, Phyllis and I had loaded our skiff on the narrow-gauge railway, which was the only transportation over White Pass. The coal-fueled train had taken the better part of a day to wind up the pass and over into Whitehorse. Now, we sped along the gravel highway in a four-wheel-drive jeep and arrived there in a matter of hours.

We towed the Lund—an eighteen-foot, V-hulled aluminum skiff—and kayak behind the jeep. As I watched the scenery of aspen and birch I began to wonder what it would be like for Phyllis and me to be on the Yukon again after so many years had passed. So much had happened since we had shared that first experience. What had Phyllis been doing the past forty-two years? I knew that my life had taken a course that I wouldn't have imagined. What about Phyllis? How would it be for us to be together for two weeks? Would we still have anything in common? Would there be anything to talk about? I was nervous. I had probably only seen Phyllis three times since she left Alaska, although we tried some years to stay in touch via Christmas cards. So much of the world had changed since those days.

The jeep wound its way up White Pass, where the gold rush of 1898 had taken off. My thoughts were on the past forty-some years. So many things had happened to me. I would never have guessed my life would turn out the way it had. The Yukon had merely whetted my appetite for adventure. That trip was the beginning of the forty years of thrill seeking I had done since.

After the Yukon River trip Phyl and I worked in Anchorage at the military base until we had enough money for another trip. This time we hiked from Wasilla, forty miles north of Anchorage, to the Richardson Highway, about 300 miles. In 1942, there was no road connecting Anchorage and Fairbanks, only the railway. But the army had begun surveying the way for what would become the Glenn Highway. Phyllis and I spent three weeks trekking that part of Alaska that would eventually be open to automobile traffic, connecting Alaska, the Yukon, British Columbia, and the lower forty-eight states. Remember that Alaska was only a territory then, as was Hawaii.

When we met the highway at Copper Center, we hitched a ride with the mail truck to Valdez. There we worked aboard a mail boat for our passage from Valdez to Cordova. Phyllis and I had a short career as mail workers. It lasted only until we arrived in Cordova a day later. (In the 1980s in Southeast Alaska, I returned to my short-lived postal career as I carried the mail sacks from the Gustavus airport to the post office. The delivery was less than a half mile in a fancy four-wheel-drive vehicle.) Phyllis had training as a beautician, but because we were dressed like rugged backpackers, we decided the best place to try our luck at jobs was in the cannery, three miles out of town. Phyllis had the opportunity to work as a flunky in the kitchen, while I had the notable title of "capper." That meant that I laid the lids on the salmon cans before they went through the sealer machine. They hardly seemed like jobs.

The first three nights in our new dwelling, a cabin up the boardwalk from the cannery, proved to be rather interesting. On the first night, Phyl and I had just bedded down when we heard yelling and screaming that went on for some time. Finally we learned that an Indian woman had given birth on the boardwalk and had been carted off to town with her newborn!

The next night we heard yelling and screaming again. We were curious, so after awhile we got up to find out what the commotion was this time. Well, it turned out that a drunk had decided he could walk on water, and in his attempt to follow Jesus he had drowned in the lagoon.

On the third night we had again just gone to bed, and again we heard yelling and screaming, what seemed to be a wild drinking party. After awhile, we heard someone stomping and storming up the boardwalk toward our cabin. Terrified, I leapt the fifteen feet across the room and into Phyllis's bed! We heard a knock on the door, or rather, a pounding. We meekly asked who it was. A low voice replied that it was Nelson, the superintendent of the cannery. He sounded upset, rather short, and wanted to know if we could cook. Apparently half the camp had gotten drunk including the cooks, and he needed someone to get started on breakfast, if there was to be any food for the crew of seventy-five workers in a few hours.

Phyl and I became overnight cooks and worked the rest of the season preparing three squares a day for up to one hundred workers. Our meat came as a side of beef; we had to do all the butchering ourselves. The only way to keep food was to store it in the "cool room," a pantry-like room with a stream running underneath it. Mind you, in those days there were no refrigerators, freezers, dishwashers, or the conveniences we now consider necessities. Phyl and I worked there all summer, taking afternoon walks and swims for recreation. (Now on a job, I take a nap in the afternoons.) The summer came to an abrupt end on one of these hikes, when I fell off a cliff, breaking my leg and collarbone and injuring my head.

I had fallen onto the beach. A fisherman heard Phyl calling and came in with a boat mattress and took me to Cordova on his boat. An army truck met us at the dock to take me to the hospital. By this time, obviously in shock, I was apparently singing "Roll Out the Barrel." My friend Tex heard me and followed us to the hospital. The hospital attendants left me alone for awhile in the emergency room. When I started having convulsions, Tex took over for the doctor who must have left me for dead. I eventually pulled through, but only after a three-month stay in the hospital.

Cordova continued to be home even after the fishing season closed. Phyl and I took a little apartment, and to keep us going we set up a darkroom in the kitchenette and did photo developing. I had worked for a time in a Juneau photo studio and both of us had worked in a studio on the military base in Anchorage, so we figured we were both profession-als! It worked out pretty well, and we were able to pay for our keep the next several months.

That spring we went south to visit family and spent a few months in California before returning to Alaska for the summer work season. Once again, Phyllis and I were a pair. During the summers of '43 and '44 we worked on Shuyak Island, a cannery site near Kodiak in the Gulf of Alaska. In the summer of '45 I returned to Kodiak without Phyllis and went to cook at a cannery in Ouzinkie on Spruce Island. That year Phyllis cooked for crews on the Alaska Railroad.

In the fall of '45 I married Gene whom I had met in Shuyak a few years earlier. We pulled in a few witnesses off the street and were married by a Russian Orthodox priest in his home; that was that. Gene and I took a bus trip to Fairbanks for our honeymoon on the recently opened Glenn Highway, the same route that Phyllis and I had hiked several years before. The bus ride was luxurious compared to the three weeks Phyllis and I spent hiking three hundred miles loaded down with packs.

Back in Anchorage, Phyllis managed a few days off her railway job and we all toured Anchorage together. Gene and I returned to Shuyak Island to spend two winters in Port Williams. Phyllis returned to California that winter and didn't visit Alaska again until 1983, when she came up for our Yukon re-run. Gene and I alternated between Shuyak Island and Juneau from 1945 to 1952. Our first two children were born in 1948 and 1951. Sometimes I would stay in Juneau while Gene went back to Shuyak to work the fishing season. My brother and his family lived in Juneau, so that was home to me.

In 1952, Gene and I packed up the kids and moved to Washington State. I don't know why, but one day it just seemed like the thing to do. For the next fifteen years, we lived in Seattle and Stanwood and raised our family, which by 1956 had grown to three children. When our youngest boy, Sheldon, was nine years old, we bought a forty-two-foot sailboat and moved aboard. Our daughter, Dorothy, was eighteen at the time and had just begun college at Western Washington State College in Bellingham, Washington. We just had the two boys then, and Bob, the eldest, was fourteen.

For a year we lived aboard our new home, and the four of us toured the San Juan Islands of Washington. A year later, in September, 1967, we set sail for the Hawaiian Islands on our ketch rig named the "Wanderer." I suppose we weren't a common family. We had sold our home and reduced our trappings to boat-size, taken the boys out of school (they studied by correspondence), and set sail for a few years in the Pacific. And really, we were novice sailors! I guess ignorance truly can be blissful. The first leg of our trip to Honolulu took us forty-one days. I remember Bob's comment when he first caught sight of the islands: "That can't be Hawaii, there's snow on the mountain!" But it was Hawaii, and we had made it!

For the next few years we sailed, stopping off and on to work. We toured the islands of Majuro, Ponape, Mokil, Truk, Guam, and the little ones in between. We spent Christmas of 1970 in Guam, and the boys and I stayed there until 1973. During that time Gene and I divorced. I suppose that a few years on a small boat will put any relationship to the test. Our eldest son, Bob, was eighteen when we arrived in Guam, and he took to doing charters on the "Wanderer." I managed a small hotel while Sheldon went back to school for a year.

The three of us moved to Hawaii in 1973. I stayed there until the summer of '75, when I returned to my first love— Alaska. It felt like a real homecoming when I found work as a cook, this time at Snug Harbor on the Alaska Peninsula. Yes, another cannery! It had been almost twenty-five years since I had lived in Alaska, and boy was it great to be back! The next year I went to work for a friend running an inn at Elfin Cove, seventy miles west of Juneau and accessible only by charter plane, or boat if you owned one. I worked at the Elf Inn for Paul Johnson for four summers. Later, it was that same Paul with whom I started the Yukon re-run trip.

During the winters I traveled, visiting friends and relatives in Washington, California and Hawaii. In 1977 I bought a small parcel of land in Gustavus near Juneau, and by 1978 I had built myself a small but very comfortable home there. I have lived in that town of two or three hundred (and growing rapidly) ever since, taking little trips here and there, still adventuring.

As we drove in the jeep to Whitehorse, I looked back on these intervening forty years with some hesitation, hoping they hadn't created a distance between Phyllis and me that would be impossible to cross. I never would have thought that we would end up back together again on the Yukon River. Phyllis had gone back to northern California where we had both grown up. She married and raised her family there. I didn't really know much of what she had done over the past four decades, but I guessed we would catch up on all that when I saw her in Dawson. I could hardly wait to see her and be on our way.

Several boats on the Yukon at Whitehorse and a young native boy who wanted to join us.

The Scookum loaded on a flat bed train car.

4

Trail of the Gold Rush:
White Pass and Beyond

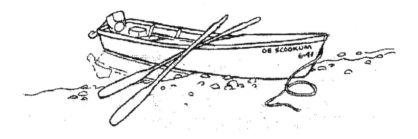

Soon the historic town of Skagway, and the awe-inspiring snow-capped divide behind the town, were in sight. This place held plenty of thrills for Phyl and me, especially after all the fabulous stories we'd heard about Skagway in the rip-roaring gold rush days. Before the war, it was just a small town of memories in one of the most breathtakingly beautiful settings imaginable.

After beaching the boat, we walked over to the Golden North Hotel, where we felt definitely conspicuous with our overalls and windblown hair. But after what we'd been through who could expect to look like a lady? And how we did enjoy the luxury of a hot bath! Our next move was to wire friends in Juneau: "WE'RE BOTH FINE AND WON'T STOP NOW." We then had our motor repaired (or so we thought) and new boards put into the boat to replace our makeshift patchwork before getting on the train to Whitehorse.

For sheer splendor of scenery, I doubt if the White Pass & Yukon Railroad can be equaled anywhere in the world. The narrow-gauge track started near the end of the long wharf, from whence the train puffed up Broadway, Skagway's main street, and began its laborious climb up the steep grade to the summit and the international boundary.

From the train one could still see the dim outline of the old trail which was used by the thousands of gold seekers as they stampeded into the newly discovered Klondike diggings. The gold rush trail of '98! We gazed at it from the train window, enthralled by thoughts of its fascinating history, absorbed in its mystery and the drama and tragedy of those hardy pioneers who had trekked up its long steep slopes, lured by dreams of gold. It seemed almost impossible that human beings could have moved supplies and mining equipment over that trail, through winter snows as deep as twenty feet or more and temperatures down to forty below. But we had talked to sourdoughs who had followed the trail of '98. Those who had lived through the ordeal seemed not to regret it.

We were glad enough to have the little engine for motive power across that rigorous trail! The thought of that trip afoot would have given pause even to our rash, youthful spirits. As our train of six cars and the small, jolting, puffing engine crawled along the narrow ledges with vertical, overhanging cliffs, we were shown several white crosses where workmen had been killed and were buried by their fellows during the construction of the famous railroad.

The crew on our train were a hardy, jolly bunch who knew a story for every bend and tunnel of the scenic route. One of the favorites was about the time when a car had broken from the main train, several lives being lost in the ensuing crash. That car happened to be carrying a large amount of liquor. A crew member had crawled on hands and knees, so they told us, down the death-dealing canyon walls, looking for an unbroken bottle. The only bottle to escape the wholesale breakage happened to be full of Coca Cola! So, after such a deal from fate, the luckless searcher didn't even bother to crawl back up the cliff!

Tomboys at heart, and out for fun, we rode in every car on the train, including the locomotive. At noon the train stopped and we enjoyed a real Northern lunch with the crew at the large station mess. There, on those wind-swept shores of Lake Bennett, most of the stampeders to the Klondike had built boats for the long river trip down to Dawson and Forty Mile. We were thrilled anew just thinking that we, four decades later, were actually following the trail of those intrepid pioneers. When crossing the summit we could see where the waters of the steep divide ran both north and south, into Canada and Alaska, within a few feet of each other. At Miles Canyon the train was stopped so that we could see the only bridge—a footbridge—across the mighty Yukon River.

Whitehorse was a very busy little town, due to a military project that was under way and to freighting on the river into the Interior. There we saw what many girls have dreamed of, members of the famous Royal Canadian Mounted Police. But, despite all we'd heard and read about those strong, illustrious men, we were somewhat disappointed when we found they weren't wearing the scarlet jackets we'd expected.

Our voyage nearly came to a dead end in Whitehorse. We had never stopped to think that a couple of girls on such a journey might be looked upon with suspicion. Both the immigration officials and the Royal Canadian Mounted Police thought, I'm sure, that we were both a little insane. They tried every means at their disposal to dissuade us from continuing our trip, but after some fast talking, we seemed to convince them that we knew what we were doing. As a matter of fact, we told them that they would either have to put up with us or let us go on our way. They decided to let us go.

By noon the next day we were on our own, with the O. B. Scookum launched on the headwaters of the Yukon. We were in seventh heaven! The sky was unbelievably blue, with huge, white, billowy clouds floating aloft. The hills and mountains were resplendent in their autumn colors of mingled red and gold and green. I doubt that I shall ever see a more magnificent sight! In some places the thick spruce trees reached right down to the water's edge, so close you could almost reach out and touch them. What a life, drifting lazily down the river, watching the blue-green water twisting and churning in big whirlpools. The motor, which was completely worn out, proved of little use, so we used our oars to steer around the bends and rocks.

Except for a few deserted cabins, there were no signs of civilization along this section of the river, yet. We felt sorry for the millions of people rushing around on crowded city streets. With so much room in the world, and so much beauty, why would anyone live in crowded, dirty surroundings?

Our lusty songs echoed from the distant mountains and cliffs, until we had to admit that the melodies of the birds were more pleasing to listen to.

Grandma

5

Grandma's Village

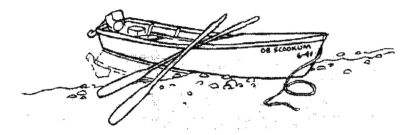

On the second day out, we came to Lake Laberge. This thirty-two-mile stretch of wild, churning water made even Lynn Canal seem calm. White waves, easily ten or twelve feet high, careened across the lake at a dizzying speed and slapped against the shore with a resounding thud. Phyl and I took one look at the angry whitecaps and decided, then and there, to make camp for the night. After much struggle with tarp, ropes, and stakes, we got our shelter up; but it didn't afford much protection from the screeching wind. Preparing our supper that night was a hard, tiresome job. Eventually we got a campfire going and a hot meal cooking above the open fire.

But we were far from disheartened. If anything, we enjoyed our struggle with wind and waves. They seemed to unleash a funny streak in us, and we laughed loud and uproariously at our predicament. It's really the hard knocks that make an outing complete. When there's no one around to call to for help, and you have to succeed or fail by your own efforts, there's a great deal of satisfaction in your success.

The next morning, despite the storm, we tried to get to the other side of the lake; but the waves kept forcing us back toward some old pilings which had once been used as a dock. We were already too far from shore to go back, and we wouldn't have had a chance had we hit those pilings. So the only thing to do was to try for the other side. Like demons we worked for more than four hours to keep the boat balanced and out of the troughs of the steep waves. One minute we would be riding high on the crest of a wave that felt like a mountain from which we could see the lake and surrounding country for miles. The next minute we would drop between walls of green water, always hoping that the waves would keep going under and not over us. Each wave broke on the crest, and its fine spray would drench us like a tropical rain.

But we stubbornly refused to let the soaking dampen our spirits. We had no time for that! When at last, completely exhausted, we stood on the opposite shore and looked back at the water we had just crossed, we realized that the only reason we hadn't been frightened was that we were too busy trying to keep alive to think about it.

"Big wind blow. White girls no go Laberge. Kill lots white men." Thus we were greeted when we reached an Athabaskan village after hiking a mile through the woods.

Remembering stories about the Natives' ability to judge weather, we made camp nearby.

On the following day the storm continued with unabated fury, and our small tarp was scarcely enough protection against the chilling blasts and stinging sleet. So away we went, back to the village. It took a lot of explaining, but we finally managed to make the villagers understand that we hoped to stay in one of their cabins until the storm blew over. The owner of one cabin was afraid to sleep inside; she kept saying, "This house die soon." Evidently she meant that it was likely to fall down at any time.

Grandma, as she asked us to call her, was a real old-timer. She swore she was more than a hundred years old, having deduced this figure from the various events of the past which she had witnessed. We believed her! According to her story, her father had bargained with the first white men to come into the country. She told us of the bush camps they had lived in before they knew what a real cabin was; of moving from one part of the country to another wherever game was plentiful. Certain roots she told us, along with wild game, had furnished their food. We decided that the Laberge country must have supplied "good grub," as two generations of her family had lived there. She explained to us how they had built corrals and trapped or snared moose and caribou. Birds of any size were good to eat, as were rabbits, gophers, and rats. We concluded that anything that looked like meat was edible to them. Their vigor was remarkable, and we marveled at their fine, strong teeth.

The old woman's eyes were almost round, and seemed gradually to have grown closed. They were very red and looked as if they were irritated. She told us that she couldn't see very well, but the day before we left she took an old rusty shotgun off the wall and shot a grouse. No one could have been more surprised than we to see her bringing home her supper that evening! We suddenly realized what it meant to eat only when you can rustle your own grub.

There were about ten children in the village, all under twelve years of age. At first they would all run and hide when they saw us strange white girls step outside the cabin. It took two days for them to get used to us, and then there was no getting rid of them. All the children had sling shots, and it was amazing to see the variety of small birds they would kill. Unless these birds were hit in the head, the boys didn't consider themselves good shots. One lad, about four years old, came in with two birds, and as everyone praised him, he beamed like a full moon.

Most of the men of the village were away working on construction jobs, so each day the women would go out and get the fish and reset the fishnets. Others would go hunting, and still others would tend the snares. These snares were made from eagle wings and were set for gophers and rabbits. Everyone seemed to have a certain responsibility to help bring in food.

It took us awhile before we could cook our meals inside the cabin, the strong odor of which made us hesitate. We decided it must have been from the dried fish that was stored in the warm, crowded rooms. When we were finally desensitized enough to be able to cook inside, the villagers laughed and said we didn't eat "good grub." I believe they thought we were as peculiar as we thought they were! We could see them talking about us among themselves, always with smirky grins. It was quite an experience for us to be queer foreigners. They ate the white man's staples, though, and were especially fond of sugar and sweets. They wore tennis shoes and had a real passion for brightly colored cotton dresses and shirts.

The older members of the village spoke halting English and were always trying to teach it to their children. Between their native tongue and their attempts at English, the poor youngsters got badly confused. When we asked the name of the kitten, one child spoke up and said, "Cat," which he evidently considered the given name of the animal. The kitten's real name, it seemed, was "Ketchum Mouse."

While tied up at the village, we had left most of our supplies in the boat, which was only about a hundred yards from the cabin where we stayed. I had brought a folding travel iron all the way from Juneau to give to Phyllis on her twenty-second birthday, which we were to celebrate somewhere along the route. One day I discovered that it was gone. Very unhappy about the loss, and not knowing what to do, I finally confided in Grandma. She was thoroughly provoked, and thought the children had probably been playing around the boat and taken it.

Calling the children into her room, she conducted what appeared to be a regular Indian trial. She would say something and each child in turn would repeat after her—much the same as in our trials, when the witness swears to tell the truth, the whole truth, and nothing but the truth. She then asked each child in turn the same question, still in Athabaskan, and each child answered in the same frightened voice, "Me no go in white girl boat." As disgusted as we were over our loss, neither Phyl nor I could keep from grinning over the entire affair. The old woman was so angry with them that she finally told them that whoever had taken the iron would never be a brave "chief." After a few more Indian oaths, the children were dismissed. They kept away from us once more.

Our stay of five days allowed us to go on several glorious hikes into the woods and across the mountains. One dog-team trail led up the mountains, the top of which commanded a magnificent view of the lake, guarded by a range of snow-capped peaks. The autumn leaves painted the lower slopes of the hillsides with their rich shades of reds, golds, and browns, intermingled with the brilliant evergreens.

All of life's pleasures were there in that small village; the Indians didn't seem to want anything but to be left alone. They were a very happy group, always laughing. If a thing wasn't done today, it could wait until the morrow. They couldn't understand why we were anxious for the storm to cease.

But cold as it was becoming, we could hardly believe Grandma when she said the summer was only half gone. Because the ground hadn't frozen over, it was still summer to her. It was hard for them to visualize any world but the small one in which they lived. It seemed impossible for them to understand that we were traveling nearly a thousand miles. We told Grandma that we were from California and the idea seemed incredible to her. She warned us that our mothers would not like it if they knew we were living in an Indian camp. Their love for one another was evidently deep and lasting. Old Grandma often spoke affectionately about her parents, who must have been dead for many years. She seemed very much interested in hearing about our families and the cities we lived in.

At long last the lake seemed calm enough for us to continue our voyage, so we loaded up the boat and were just about ready to shove off. Suddenly an old man, the only man who happened to be left in camp at the time, came running down the trail and begged us not to leave. He warned us that the water would get rough before the day was past. The old Indians were very superstitious about water, always calling it "hot" or "bad." Both of us were extremely eager to be on our way, but realized that the old man knew more about the dangers than we. He really got excited, motioning wildly with his hands, trying to show us how the big waves would throw us up against the rocky banks and then . . ."no more white girl." That was enough for us. As it happened, the old man was certainly correct; in a few hours the lake was rougher than ever.

We considered taking a steamer across the lake; we were told in the village that we could signal for it to stop. When the steamboat eventually hove into sight, we ran to the old Indian and asked him to stop it for us. We were so excited at the prospect of continuing our journey that our spirits were considerably dampened when he told us that the steamer could stop only on the other side of the lake. They never told us the same story twice, and were forever contradicting themselves.

After five days of warm hospitality, we left the little village with some reluctance and started our thirty-two-mile row across the lake. The weather had cleared, and the new-fallen snow on the high mountains loomed against the blue sky. We rowed steadily for eleven hours to reach our goal at the other end of the lake. The shoreline was very irregular, at times a smooth and sandy beach, then changing abruptly to sharp, treacherous rocks and cliffs. At times the lake was a perfect mirror reflecting all the beauty of winter and summer combined.

It was bitterly cold that night when we camped at the lower end of Lake Laberge. We heard the comforting chug of a wood-burning sternwheeler paddling uplake, so we knew there were others out there in the night. Imagine our dismay when we awoke the next morning and found everything frozen stiff, with about a quarter of an inch of frost covering our sleeping bags. A mosquito circled right above my face. It was the only one of the pests we saw on that entire trip.

Paul as skipper and Hal already digging in bag for a snack.

Boots resting on rail-characteristic of our basking in the heat of the day while slowly going downstream.

6

Really Living!

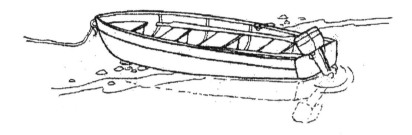

Paul, our skipper, launched the motored skiff at Whitehorse. Cynthia and Hal had brought a kayak along, and we towed that behind the Lund when we weren't using it. The friends who drove us to Whitehorse went on to Dawson, taking my kayak with them. The plan was that friends would drive to Dawson and leave a car for Paul's group to drive back to Juneau. Paul would tow the Lund back with him and I would assemble my collapsible kayak and meet up with Phyllis.

The narrow Lewes River carried us about thirty miles from Whitehorse into Lake Laberge. The sun was bright and warm and we relaxed, but with an alert eye. The river is about 400 to 500 feet wide and dotted with many small islands and channels that can lead to dead ends.

We made several stops and found an endless assortment of wildflowers: ladyslipper orchids in great patches, their small heads bowed as if to shade their pretty faces from the glaring sun; juniper berries, grey-blue berries on a creeping evergreen shrub (gin, anyone?); and wild raspberries in abundance. There were sweet, ripe gooseberries and larkspur . . . such a garden! But, oh, the mosquitos!!! They were enjoying the day too!

Crossing Lake Laberge with the group was a snap. The outboard—well, motors must have improved over the years; this one was dependable. Without incident, we made it to a small island two thirds of the way across the lake, where we stopped for the day. The three tents were soon set up, blue, gold and red, spaced in the trees. It was a comfortable camp with good equipment and all the comforts.

It was such a good day! This was nearly a month earlier than the first trip, and a hot day it was! Some of the group had gone off paddling in the kayak while I rowed the skiff quietly, and others napped. But just being there again made me too happy to even close my eyes. I loved every minute of it. I began to think about the many changes in this river that I had been so anxious to get back to. All these past years I had held memories of cabins along the way where Phyl and I were so warmly welcomed by families. Our group had seen none on this day.

Now the wood-burning sternwheelers were no longer running, so there was no need for the woodcutters along the way. In earlier days, the cordwood had been stacked on the riverbank, convenient for loading, so we could always spot a settlement easily. I kept looking for a familiar sight. Even though it was so peaceful, I felt a twinge of loneliness thinking of how the river life would never be the same again. I would have liked to have gone ashore and looked for remains of the old Athabaskan village whose hospitality had thoroughly warmed us when we were so young and inexperienced. But when you are traveling with a group and the motor is running—well, you just go on.

After our day on the river we had a good hot meal. The beach wood was dry so there was no problem getting a fire going. The men went fishing and the gals wrote in their journals. Later I tried to float on my air mattress which didn't really hold me, so I had a good swim. The water wasn't too cold.

I rinsed my clothes out in the lake and hung them on the drift logs to dry. A great breeze was blowing but the "skeeters" were still around. The others retired to their tents early, but I sat by the campfire, toasted a few more marshmallows and had another cup of hot chocolate. A sliver of a moon was coming up over the hilltops and I was thinking of how we struggled forty-two years before to get across the upper end of that lake. The water had been so menacing then, an appropriate setting for Robert Service's spooky poem:

There on the marge of Lake Lebarge
I cremated Sam McGee.

Finally in my small tent with the screen zipped, I was comfortable and the mosquitos were frustrated. During the night a strong wind came up, and I crawled out to check my clothes on the logs. Someone had gotten up before I had and everything was well covered with tarps. The waves were whipping onto the beach and the birds were still singing. I hadn't heard such a chorus in a long time.

The group was aboard the Lund the next morning, well rested and fed, with full coffee cups. Really living!

Before we left Lake Laberge we saw the Pleistocene hills, carved by the glacial age. The view in every direction was an interesting picture. Each section was completely different, so the shutters were constantly clicking. Once again we picked up the strong scent of juniper berries. As the temperature and humidity changed, the fragrances became more acute. It seems as though most of the time we are too distracted to appreciate our sense of smell. On shore we found lowbush blueberries, the first I had seen of these; and so many wildflowers.

Carmacks — Tommy, Johnny and Phyllis

7

Birthday Bannock and Church Mug-Up

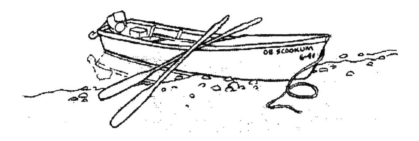

That morning, when Phyl and I awoke to find an inch of frost covering everything, we had another surprise in store for us as well. During the night one of the river steamers had gone by, and the big waves from its wake had lifted the O. B. Scookum into a shallow mud pit. By walking on logs and pulling, and by poling with the oars, we were getting the boat out inch by inch. But suddenly Phyl fell in! Knee deep in mud, she couldn't have become any colder; so she just kept on wading around in the icy water until she managed to get the skiff out to deeper anchorage. We knew there was a government telegraph station about a quarter of a mile farther on, so we didn't even bother to light a fire. That was a long, cold quarter of a mile; but our spirits were braced by the thought of hot coffee, a warm fire, and someone to talk to.

Imagine how we felt when we drew abreast of the little cabin only to find the door securely locked, and no friendly smoke issuing from the chimney. But we had been fore-warned that we would encounter plenty of grief along the Yukon. This, then, was one of those times. We consoled ourselves with the thought that the old-timers, coming along that same route in the early days, had difficulties that dwarfed ours by comparison. Lifting our voices in cheerful harmony, we rowed across the river to a sunny beach. After all, we still had a sense of humor. Time and again it came to our rescue during that long trip down the Yukon.

We lit a fire. Phyl hung her slacks and wool socks on a willow arch to dry, while I cooked hot cakes and bacon, and made coffee. (These breakfasts were the cat's meow until cholesterol was discovered.) With full tummies and dry clothes, we were able to relax and enjoy the natural beauties of Thirty Mile River, part of the headwaters of the mighty Yukon. The Thirty Mile is narrow and very swift. After the stiff row of the previous day, we were content to have the river move us along. We were amazed at the immense rocks we found ourselves drifting over. Watching the river bottom, we understood why so many crafts had been wrecked on this short section of the Yukon.

After thirty miles of drifting, we came to Hootalinqua. Here the Teslin and Thirty Mile rivers meet. This junction was once an important post for the gold seekers who came up the Stikine River and down the Teslin. There Ken Snure's cabin, which we found still standing, was a mecca for travelers. The words, "I go to Hootalinqua," were painted on the side of a weather-beaten crate. That night we camped in the half-fallen-down cabin. Through the caved-in roof we could watch from our sleeping bags as the northern lights played their wondrous symphony of color on the Yukon skies. We wondered what old-timer had built that cabin, and what had become of him. And, woman-like, we wondered if he had "struck it rich."

The next day was September 19, Phyl's twenty-second birthday. We celebrated the event with a huge bannock, baked to perfection alongside a campfire—the best one we ever made—and spread generously with homemade blueberry jam. (A bannock is a baking powder bread baked beside a campfire, using another pan angled above the bread to reflect the heat from the fire. Of course we didn't have foil in those days. That would have simplified camping!) The occasion seemed just as festive as if we had been able to change from our greasy overalls to pretty dresses and dine at a sophisticated restaurant.

Around our boat that night we found what we thought at the time to be the tracks of a huge dog. Later we learned that they must have been those of a prowling wolf.

Big Salmon, the next settlement on the river, was deserted. At that point the steamer "Whitehorse" passed us, and everyone aboard waved in hearty greeting, just as if they'd known us all our lives. That's the way people are up in the big North country—cordial and friendly at all times.

The next stop we made was at a bar on the river, where a man and his wife had a sluice box set up. They would prospect with their gold pans, and whenever they found a promising spot, they would shovel the pay dirt into the sluice box. The gold was then recovered from the mats inside the box. We had never seen such an operation before and were very much interested.

What a treat to have someone to talk to! That night we unrolled our sleeping bags outside their tent. Although it snowed most of the night, we were quite comfortable beside the two blazing logs of the campfire. When we woke at six o'clock the next morning, the couple served us boiled (not instant!) coffee in our sleeping bags!

Our food supplies were running low, and the weather was still bad. We stopped next at a wood camp and slept in the supply room. We slept on the two wooden bunks with no mattress, but there was a roof over our head, and we were dry. The men at the camp were wonderful cooks, and I do believe they had every kind of can opener ever invented. They also had a battery radio, and we heard real music again, after the uncertain pleasure of our own singing.

The men worked on our outboard motor, but to no avail. They finally gave it up as hopeless, but insisted that we use theirs as far as Carmacks, fifty miles downriver. We had hopes of having our own repaired there. They were surely good to us! And they seemed especially surprised that we should be making such a long journey by ourselves. They couldn't seem to understand why we got a kick out of it.

They told us how the old sourdoughs holed in for the winter. It seems the old-timers had little to do but survive during the long, cold winter months, so they arranged to have as much comfort as possible. A true sourdough, the woodmen told us, had his bed within easy reach of his stove. Instead of cutting his wood into short lengths, he shoved in a long log, inching it in as the end burned off, and never left his bed. If he was exceptionally lazy, he arranged it so that all his cooking could be done almost entirely from his bed. I suppose we believed them. They told us a lot of other stories too, until we hardly knew what to believe.

After a few more exhortations to "be careful," we left for Carmacks. The borrowed motor helped our speed, but we missed the warmth that rowing imparted. Since we had left Juneau, Phyl and I had lost many inches around the midriff. Rowing was a wonderful pastime and great exercise! (To think how much people pay to have the modern indoor rowing machines now so they can exercise and watch television at the same time! Then we had all the exercise we could want *and* the beauty and tranquility to boot.)

About two hours after leaving the wood camp, we saw smoke ahead. Then we didn't see it. Then we did. We were puzzled. Finally we reached an old mission at Little Salmon and found two young fellows who had been prospecting in the nearby hills. They had moved an old stove inside the mission and made themselves comfortable. When they heard our motor, they had hastily carried the stove outside. When our motor died, they took the stove in again. They were anxious about being caught in the church without permission. Quite a game.

Phyl and I could see no harm in keeping warm and drinking coffee inside a church, especially since it was Sunday. So we all stoked up a good fire and made ourselves comfortable. I don't know who was more surprised—the two young men at seeing us, or we at seeing them! They'd been having their troubles too, and it was like old home week with us sitting around exchanging experiences.

It turned out the fellows, Tommy and Johnny, had been traveling and trapping for three years. They started at Great Slave Lake in the Canadian Northwest Territories, then went through the Nahanni country, and eventually came down the Little Salmon River to the Yukon River. Tommy and Johnny told us that the birds had all gone south, and the berries were gone, so it must be time to go back to civilization and go to work. All this time the guys had been hanging onto a pair of Florsheim dress shoes—just in case the occasion ever arose!

After a "mug-up," they decided to go along as far as Carmacks with us. Everything went fine until the motor sputtered and stopped. Out of gas! Well, it could be worse, we knew. We still had the oars, and it wasn't much farther.

There was a roadhouse at the river settlement of Carmacks; Phyl and I enjoyed a fine meal and comfortable sleeping accommodations, for a change. Of course they had running water—all you had to do was run down to the creek after it. Tommy, Johnny, Phyl and I helped cook. We also pulled carrots from the garden—bushels of them—and stored them for winter use as both human and horse feed. We were impressed by the luxuriance of the large gardens, which seemed to be everywhere. Vegetables grew to phenomenal size, and they surely did taste good to us after having eaten nothing but canned vegetables for a long time. We made carrot pies and even carrot biscuits! They were great! (If dehydrated or freeze-dried foods were available at that time we never knew about them; but we probably couldn't have afforded them anyway. Between Phyl and me we had less than $300 to get from Juneau to Anchorage.)

We spent the evening gathered around the big table at the roadhouse, hearing more stories about the earlier days told by the old man who operated the place. We stayed in Carmacks the next day while our motor was being over-hauled, and we bought a fresh supply of food and gas. Our five-gallon gas can only held four Canadian gallons and that took a bit of figuring out. We got quite a kick out of choosing among the different food brands on the shelves. All of them were Canadian, and all unfamiliar to us. Even the money was Canadian. The prices were somewhat higher than we were accustomed to, but by the time the exchange on our American money was figured out, we came out about even.

On the following morning we waved farewell to Johnny and Tom, the two young prospectors, and shoved off downstream. The motor had purred like a charm when we were warming it up on the beach, but it wouldn't give so much as a sputter once we got out on the river. With a sigh we picked up the oars.

8

Old Relics

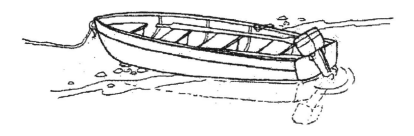

It was a day of kayaking and just drifting after our group got off Lake Laberge at about eleven in the morning. It had taken longer than I had expected. Phyllis and I had rowed the length of it in eleven hours with no shore stops. But this time the lake was boiling and we just wanted to get off of it. With the motor running it took four or five hours total, moving at an economical speed. (We carried extra gas and oil mixture, not knowing how often it would be available.)

The Thirty Mile River at the lake's outlet was very swift, and though the water was clear on the first trip, now it was a mess, full of pollution! We had left Whitehorse with five and a half gallons of fresh water, and it was fortunate that we had. In the good old days, we hadn't needed to carry water.

Quietly drifting along one afternoon, somewhat dopey from snoozing in the hot sun, we were surprised by a visitor.

"Look! What's that, way up there? See it? No, over there!"

"Oh, yes, it's a bear! And it's a big one, must be a grizzly!"

By now everyone was wide awake, watching the bear as it came slowly down a gully on the mountainside. "It's a big one, but I don't think it's a grizzly. It's a blackie." Well, when it finally got down to the river's edge, the bear turned out to be a porcupine! Had the hot sun and solitude of the river affected us that much?

Near Hootalinqua we spotted the old sternwheeler "Evelyn." The territory was reconditioning a lot of these old relics for historical purposes. I mentioned to my companions that it was interesting something more than sixty years old was still hanging around. "Well, look who's talking!" was the response. I was sixty-two years old then, remembering with disbelief that the last time I was here was on Phyllis's twenty-second birthday.

The riverbanks along here were most interesting— great ramparts alive with swallows darting in and out of their homes. Eagles also inhabited the tops of the cliffs. The log cabins along here, probably occupied in 1941, were now beyond use.

I looked anxiously for the church at Little Salmon. I was still disappointed that the river had changed so much; I kept looking for familiar sights. Nora and I walked along the shoreline and found the old cemetery with the "spirit houses." Such a lot of love and work had gone into these at one time, but customs and values had changed, and generations had moved on, leaving these uncared for. Hopefully they served their purpose by consoling loved ones at the time. Dolls and toys and perhaps some tools or utensils had been left at the burial site and were scattered about.

There were a lot of homes, buildings, and ongoing construction below Little Salmon, with survey markers and roads coming in. We even met a car on the highway! We camped across the river above Carmacks, thankful for a gentle breeze and deep, soft moss to put our tents on. The next morning we headed toward town.

This was perhaps the prettiest section of the trip so far. The riverbanks were great carved cliffs riddled with swallows' homes, and the birds came and went endlessly. Big, beautiful, fluffy clouds created great cloud shadows on the green velvet hills. The contrasting shades of greens, greys and golds was such a grand display of Mother Nature! We noticed a natural arch in the limestone, weird castles and imaginary figures. The shadows and colors continued to change rapidly and I couldn't stop watching for the next magic appearance!

As we motored into Carmacks we could see power lines crossing the river here and there. The Yukon is a popular navigation aid for pilots, so the power lines had large white balls attached to them to warn low-flying planes. We passed under a huge bridge at Carmacks—new, of course, since Phyl and I had been there. The town was bustling, quite a contrast from 1941. There were gas stations, a laundromat, a hotel and several stores. We bought a few things and tended to the essentials—hot showers!

While Nora and Cynthia shopped and the guys drank beer, I walked around town, drifting toward nostalgia. I wished I could go back to the good old days when everything was much more personal, when a stop in a riverside town was like a visit with family. But I snapped out of that mood when we got back to the boat and found the guys fast asleep in the sun; amazing what a little Canadian beer can do.

Biederman family saying good-bye after our weekend visit with them.

The owners of the tent where we saw gold dust and nuggets in fruit jars and grocery boxes for chairs—a paradise of their own.

A man and his dogs on the bank of the river.

9

River Folks

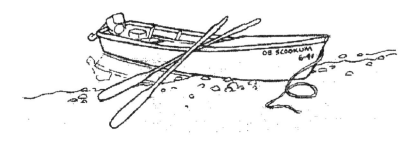

Five Finger Rapids soon loomed ahead, and Phyllis and I perked up for the thrill of thrills. There the shores rise in steep, sheer, rock walls, and four huge boulders rise at intervals across the water, splitting it into five separate channels, or "fingers." Only one of the channels is navigable. We kept to the right, as so many people had exhorted us to do. Phyl had the oars, so I took several quick snapshots as we shot through the swift, narrow passage. It was exciting all right, but it was over all too quickly. We had looked forward with eagerness to Five Finger Rapids as the high spot of our big adventure, and we found ourselves regretting that it was over.

We stopped for lunch on an island overlooking the statuesque boulders of the rapids, and as we ate, we discussed our next river challenge—Rink Rapids, only about five miles downriver. Some had warned us that Rink Rapids were even more treacherous than the notorious Five Fingers. After washing our lunch dishes in the river, and repacking our camp equipment, we started eagerly for the next adventure. While I was contemplating the dangers, Phyl came out with one of her characteristic bon mots. "Oh well, Mary," she philosophized. "Don't take life too seriously, because we don't get out of it alive, anyway."

Rink Rapids did toss us around considerably. There were rocks everywhere. It was an exciting ride, but the O. B. Scookum came through with flying colors. What a boat! We were proud of Scooky that day.

At Yukon Crossing, Phyl and I inspected the remains of the old roadhouse and police post buildings—derelicts of an earlier era. In one of the buildings we found a stove and good shelter and managed to do a small washing. Nor could we resist spending an hour watching the gorgeous sunset reflected on the east side of the river.

By the aid of our flashlight—which sometimes worked, but more often didn't after so many duckings in the water (I don't think waterproof flashlights were available then)—we made our way down the riverbank for a bucket of water late that evening. All around our boat were huge bear tracks! It made us a little bit jittery knowing that such wild animals could come and go without announcing their presence. But we didn't waste time worrying about what we'd do if we met a bear or a wolf face to face.

Bright and early the next morning we were off to a good start. But the exhilaration of the sunshine and fresh air was too much for Phyl; she forgot her own strength and broke the board which held the oarlock in place. Overboard it went, into the swift current of the fast-widening river. After several minutes of frantic chasing, we managed to catch it. We'd used most of our nails during the ordeal of Lynn Canal, but we stopped anyway and repaired the damage the best we could.

Not far from Yukon Crossing, we came upon a large attractive home where a man and wife lived with their two young children. They had a large garden, and the father had just returned from hunting for the winter's meat supply. The family penned fish in a large trap in the river and later would cut through the ice and catch whitefish. A winter freezer with no power bills to pay!

On another stop along here we met a family with two small sons, the Biedlemans. I know it was a Saturday night because the next day they went through their Sunday rituals. The father read the Sunday funnies, which had been collected the entire previous year and then read on the day nearest to that issue. Sunday was celebrated with canned grapefruit sections for breakfast and, of course, sourdough hot cakes, which were a staple all the time. We slept warm and dry in their storage shed, which still bore the unmistakable odor of pelt-drying boards.

There was no school to which the boys could go, and their mother was teaching them with the aid of a correspondence course. Each child had his own small desk. Later we were impressed to learn that the mother herself had had the opportunity for only a fourth-grade education and was studying along with her children.

[Many years later in Washington, where I was raising my family, I found an article in the pictorial section of the Sunday paper describing the life of the younger of these boys. He had gone on to become a noted engineer; he had worked on the Seattle Space Needle for the 1964 World's Fair. In 1983, we inquired about this family and learned that one son was living near Eagle, but we could not get any other information.]

Minto was our next stop. There we had lunch with an old sourdough—of '98 vintage. He lived all by himself, kept a team of horses for which he raised hay, and had a fine, intelligent dog. Phyl and dogs always made friends immediately. She had a few bits of red nail polish still left and when she petted the dog, the old man thought she had been bitten. He was actually embarrassed when she showed him it was nail polish.

The old man served us lunch. As our supplies were unusual for the "river folks," we could usually supply something that was a treat for them. In exchange for our contribution to the lunch, the old man gave us each a glass of his home-brew. He was missing a hand, and opening the bottles of beer with his prosthetic hook was quite a trick. After it was well shaken up from the struggle, the brew was quite lively. This he solved by capturing the foaming liquid in a large aluminum dishpan. How can you refuse a drink in such a situation? It was good!

After lunch in the old cabin, we adjourned to his new home for coffee. This was a fine cabin he had built up the hill overlooking the river. We were amused to learn that he hadn't quite made up his mind to move from the old cabin, where he had spent so many happy years of his life.

In the new house, we listened to the latest news over the radio. During the news broadcast the old sourdough remarked that he surely was glad he lived in the North, where everything was peaceful and orderly. He was a well-educated man, and we were sure he could have lived in luxury in some large city. But instead he whiled away the time between his two log cabins on the quiet bank of the Yukon. He was rich by our standards.

From Minto there was a wagon road that covered the hundred miles to Mayo, hub of the great Yukon silver district. Later we heard that the last steamer of the season had been unable, because of low water, to make the trip up the Stewart River to the silver metropolis. With its cargo of provisions and supplies, it was forced back to Stewart City, leaving the town of Mayo facing a shortage. Most of those supplies were taken back to Dawson, and flown over to Mayo at a cost of sixteen cents a pound! [It is odd now to remember how devastating it was for residents to pay that freight charge. Nowadays I often pay forty cents a pound to get something flown out to my home in Gustavus, only fifty miles from Juneau. Things do change—river life and air rates.]

Surveying the high banks and watching the bird life ashore.

Hot sun... Beer and gas prices—too much!!

10

Landscapes

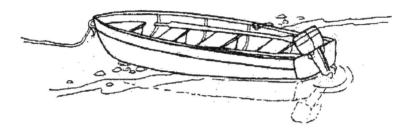

Before leaving Carmacks, Paul refilled our gas jugs at $2.10 a gallon, and my old journal reminds me of how shocked Phyl and I had been at having to pay almost a dollar for an imperial gallon in 1941! It was probably about fifteen cents a gallon in Juneau at the time. Time goes on. After a hot meal we drifted on down the river. For a minute I thought we were going upstream—impossible—but here the contour of the river almost circles back to Carmacks.

The old roadhouse where Phyllis and I had stayed was still standing about a mile downriver. Oddly, the first thing I recalled was the real damask linen tablecloths that had been used for sheets. I was disappointed when my group vetoed the idea of stopping for a peek. After several years of traveling alone there are disadvantages to having companions, as dear as they might be. Traveling alone, I stop at the merest excuse.

With the Lund and outboard we were traveling about fifteen miles per hour. We expected to cover in two weeks what had taken Phyl and me five. But neither Phyl nor I had been strapped by other duties, as business-bound folks are today. In 1941 we were rich in time, though certainly not rich in money!

Five Finger Rapids lay ahead; we could hear the roar. The rapids are a short distance of good fast water in a narrow passage between four towering boulders. Early steamers had cables ashore to winch them upstream in the channel that was safest. Our group could see remains of the cable aid station that still stood. There is a highway lookout stop on the west side, but who wants to see it from a car? Friends have taken a photo from there and sent it to me with the caption, "Mary and Phyllis went through THAT in a rowboat!"

Hal and Cynthia very carefully boarded the kayak that we had drawn up alongside the Lund and secured themselves with life jackets and spray skirts. Paddles in position, they were let loose and away they went. It was a short fast ride but it looked like fun. The kayak was towed back upstream and Paul and Hal rode it next. I believe all of us regretted that it didn't last longer. Rink Rapids provided the next inviting moment. We stopped to taxi the kayak back up a few times so everyone could get a piece of the action. It was fun in the Lund, too!

Soon we saw a big slide of ash on the river caused by a volcanic eruption over a thousand years ago in the Wrangell-

St. Elias Mountains. Locals had named the slide "Sam McGee's Ashes"; he must have been a big man!

That day Paul and Hal kayaked ahead and Nora, Cynthia and I drifted in the skiff. The sun was out, but since we were all rather burned from sun and wind, we rotated to keep our faces shaded. We spared no sun bloc, but Nora was the smartest with her bandana over her nose, looking like a bank robber most of the time.

We drifted past a long slide area, where the bank was about 200 feet high with brilliantly colored ribbons of scree that displayed years and years of erosion—a geologist's dream.

The kayak was about a quarter of a mile ahead of us, but sounds carried so well across the water that we could plainly hear the voices of the men. Drifting in the aluminum boat, we could hear the sand rolling along on the underside. The river was deep here, but the flow of the water kept the sand suspended. Of course this constant movement of tons of soil explained why the river's course was forever changing, a never-ending challenge for the river pilots.

While snapping pictures around the campfire one morning, I dropped my camera and of course it sprang open, causing some pictures to be lost. The camera seemed to be doomed on this trip. A few days earlier it had slipped off my lap into the bilge water. We had taken the film out and left the camera open to dry it as much as possible. Later that day we had heard an unfamiliar beeping and each of us looked with surprise and suspicion at the others, soon to realize that the battery had shorted out from the moisture and was letting us know. Sounds that would go unnoticed in the busy worka-day world were so startling in the quiet of the river!

One night we clambered up a high bank to camp in a pleasant grove of birch trees. Cynthia said she'd scream in disgust if she found any more evidence of careless campers, disappointingly common on this trip. Forty-two years earlier, Phyllis and I had not come upon any old campsites, as there was very little traffic on the river except for the boats of people who actually lived in the area. Phyl and I had been told that we were "the first two gals to travel it alone," but we had no proof. Today, there were many telltales of the frequent traveler, and our birch grove proved no exception. As promised, Cynthia screamed in disgust before we returned to the boat to get our gear. I was thankful that the younger ones were respectful of the older one and carried all the equipment up to the campsite.

A high bluff was our home for the night. The winds whipped our tents dry and freed them of needles and twigs that we had carried inside. My tent smelled fresh and I slept wonderfully. I was close to the edge of the bank and could hear the coyotes yelping across the river. The next morning Hal reported that he had gotten a great picture of the full moon across the Yukon, and the rest of us were sorry he hadn't wakened us.

As we continued down the river, fish camps were appearing more often. Racks were loaded with drying salmon—winter provisions for people and dog teams alike. But we ate peanut butter sandwiches, cold wieners, beer nuts and fresh nectarines. I threw the pits ashore hoping a miracle would make them grow. The rose hips along here were broken open and covered with an odd pollen that attracted the bees. Usually the bright red fruits are healthy and fun to eat, but we were not tempted by the ones we saw.

It was sunset when we reached Yukon Crossing, thus named because it was where the winter overland trail crossed the river. Now that planes dominated transportation in the northland, the old wagon and sled trails were practically abandoned. Most of the smaller villages along the river received mail by air each week during the winter, while the river steamers carried mail and freight during the short summer months.

As we traveled along in the Lund, a flock of tiny white plovers with green wings were rocking back and forth on their wiry legs, balancing on the rocks at the edge of the current. They reminded me of the bird that picks up toothpicks at my friend's house. Sights such as this, so foreign to city dwellers, seemed to make the journey enjoyable for my companions. Seeing their satisfaction eased the regret I often felt that my younger friends missed knowing the earlier days of the Yukon Territory.

In Minto Flats the rocks were alive with swallows flitting in and out of their homes. The rock terraces were covered with lichen and flowers, a beautiful natural landscaping. On one high rocky bluff I watched intently until I was quite positive I had sighted some Dall sheep. I asked Paul to "check out those white rocks up there," and he confirmed that there were indeed eight sheep. The eight sheep and the five travelers studied each other for several seconds and then as the mountain residents decided all was well, they laid their heads down once more, and we drifted on.

The sun was unusually bright, bringing out sunglasses and changes at the helm. I did hope that the blue, blue sky and cumulus white clouds were adding a lot to our pictures.

A peaceful day on the river.

11

Yukon Hospitality

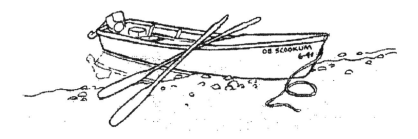

Four hours of rowing took us to the Pelly River, where it joined the Lewes River to form the main Yukon. Although all the distance we had covered from Lake Laberge was termed the Yukon, this junction of the Pelly and Lewes marked the place where the headwaters ended and the mighty river began. The name "Yukon," we were told, derived from "Youcon," a Kutchin word meaning "big," or "powerful."

At the junction we crossed the river to the old trading post of Fort Selkirk. There the Hudson's Bay Company operated a trading post until 1852, when the Chilkat Indians raided the place and burned the buildings. Fort Selkirk was rebuilt as a mission in 1892 and experienced some growth as a Royal Canadian Mounted Police post during the gold rush. When Phyl and I came through, there were quite a few Athabaskans living there and only a few white people. In addition to the RCMP headquarters, the village consisted of a general store and government telegraph office.

Phyl and I were welcomed by the wife of the Mountie stationed at Selkirk. She had learned by way of the government telephone system that we were coming, and she took us into her home with unsurpassed hospitality. We ate a delicious hot dinner—the first moose steaks we'd tasted—and we slept in the comfort of a real bed! We even had hot baths in a folding rubber tub! Such luxury and such kindness we certainly hadn't expected. The couple's daughter was attending school in Dawson, so we stayed in her room, quite fascinated with the snowshoe rabbits mounted on the wall.

We hadn't been under way long the next day when we spotted a moose. But it saw us too and departed before we could get a snapshot. Farther down the river we met an Athabaskan family. They were "lining" their boat upstream, pulling it from the shore by ropes tied to bow and stern.

That same day we came upon an Indian fellow who had just shot a moose. He had cleverly tracked it to the water's edge, shooting it there and saving himself the work of carrying it out of the forest. He promised to meet us the next day and give us some fresh steaks.

Soon after that we got stuck high and dry on a sandbar. Phyl had already had more than her share of wading, so I jumped out and dragged the skiff out into the channel again.

We reached Isaac Creek just as dusk was settling over the river. Judging from the old buildings which were still standing, Isaac Creek must have been another busy place during the boom days of the Klondike. With our usual curiosity, we took the flashlight and in its feeble light we investigated the collapsing structures. It wasn't much help. Just as we would crawl through a broken window and stumble over a pile of old harnesses, boots, and other discarded equipment, the light would go out. More than ever we wondered what had become of the stampeders who had once occupied these decaying buildings.

Our Indian friend, true to his promise, overtook us the next morning. We lost no time in cooking and eating the moose steaks. We had real bread too, which the Mountie's wife had given us. It was delicious, after having eaten bannock for so long!

That evening we watched a glorious display of northern lights. It is an indescribable feeling to relax beside a glowing campfire in the evening, watching the weird, mystic lights playing about the sky—especially in a land now almost deserted and bearing the ghostly remnants of long-gone inhabitants. We talked about the days that were gone and about the uncertain future, and it occurred to me that the campfires of the North must have heard many a life story— stories that the speaker had once promised never to tell a soul!

The next day we basked in the warm Indian-summer sun. Another day, another lap in our journey. This one brought us to Coffee Creek, where we found a large ranch. The ranchers were an elderly couple, Mr. and Mrs. Malloy, real pioneers who had come to their lonely spot on the Yukon back in the early days. Their lives had not been without excitement, and we probably heard only a few of the incidents which had crowded them.

They did tell us about the time, six years previously, when the ice had jammed in the main river and flooded them out of house and home. They had to climb the ridgepole of their cabin to escape the angry waters as they swept over the riverbank. True pioneers, the Malloys did not give up after the catastrophe. They rebuilt their home and outbuildings, and were still plugging along—no doubt much happier than most people on the "Outside," whom such misfortunes had never touched.

Morning wash up—running water!

Phyllis could always find a horse or a dog for a friend. We're leaving Brittons and their hired hand on a foggy morning.

12

Ma Britton

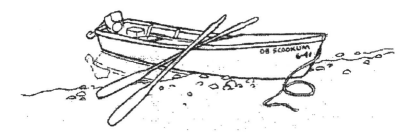

"Row, row, row your boat, gently down the stream," we sang lustily as we rowed lazily downstream that afternoon. The scenery was superb and the sky was blue and brilliant. At Kirkman Creek we stopped to visit. Our encounters with people along the river had been so intriguing that now we would stop without the slightest excuse.

Our visit with Ma and Pa Britton turned out to be one of the highlights of our trip. Ma Britton had baked bread and donuts the day we saw their "smoke" and stopped at Kirkman Creek. She invited us in and insisted that we wait for "young fellow" to return from the mine. At twilight he came down the canyon with his two-wheel chariot pulled by his faithful horse. Such a sight! "Young fella" was probably seventy years old, but he was full of enthusiasm and loved hunting for gold. Dinner with the couple was special. All of us had so much to talk about. Afterwards Ma Britton played the piano and served coffee in tiny little tea cups. Inlaid on the handle of the silver teaspoon was a tiny gold nugget.

Phyllis and I slept in a guest bunkroom, and when Ma Britton thought we were asleep she added a fur robe over us as if we were her children. As she tucked us in, I faked sleep, loving it! As Ma and Pa Britton were seeing us off the next morning, we were still thanking them when Ma Britton said, "You don't have to thank us, girlie, you've given us something to talk about all winter long!"

A heavy fog blanketed the river, but we set out anyway, rowing hard to keep warm. Around noon the fog lifted, unveiling another gorgeous Indian-summer day, with clear blue skies and golden sunshine. The autumn leaves had almost all fallen by that time, and fresh snow had crept from the larger ranges to the lower mountain peaks.

We made fast time and soon reached White River, a glacial stream. Up to that point the waters of the Yukon had been a translucent green, but there they became clouded with the milky contents of the tributary, and their beautiful clearness was gone.

Our next stop was Stewart City, located where the Stewart River flows into the Yukon, seventy-two miles above Dawson. The riverboat "Keno" was docked there and a crew member invited us to come aboard and have "tea" with the captain. We were honored so we went and were served tea and sweets in grand style! A real treat of linens, chairs and tables! Although we felt a little grubby, no one seemed to notice as they welcomed us royally.

We didn't go much farther that afternoon but camped early and cleaned the boat. We had spilled three quarts of heavy Mobil oil inside the O. B. Scookum, and she really was quite a mess. After making camp, we heated water and gave her decks a good swabbing. How shiny and clean the O. B. Scookum looked! In contrast, we were quite a mess, so we heated some river water over the campfire and washed our hair. Phyllis, the beautician on our trip, set our hair in pin curls and tied a bandana around our heads. We looked pretty sharp the next morning when we combed out our precious curls!

13

The River's Work

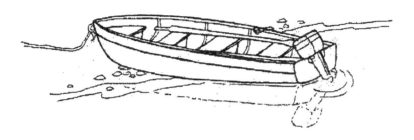

The five of us climbed up a low bank and were on a nice open plateau at Selkirk. The terrain here was sandy and dry with hardly any underbrush, but many small flowers were somehow able to flourish. Downstream, we could see the Pelly Ramparts—huge palisades of volcanic rock. It was early evening and very peaceful. There were no people around, but we could hear a generator running nearby.

Led by its sound, we reached a construction camp where the crew was having dinner. The government was rebuilding some of the historic buildings, and, with directions from the crew, we found our way to an interesting church that was nearly restored. The woodwork and stained glass windows inspired a certain silence among us. Were some of us quietly saying a prayer that our trip would continue to be safe?

We had an enjoyable visit with Danny Roberts, the town historian. Later we went on to see the military cemetery. We had to swat a path through the mosquitos to get there, but it proved worthwhile when we saw how well the cemetery had been cared for.

We headed downriver out of Selkirk, meandering past the towering pinnacles that form the Pelly Palisades. From the Lund we saw a moose cow and calf—finally! All our cameras were snapping, and I was wishing I had a telephoto lens. Afterwards, drifting along, still excited about having finally seen a moose, there was another one! Incredible! She was knee deep in the marsh and ducking her head underwater to get another mouthful of roots. As she raised her head the water dripped from her mouth and sparkled in the sunlight. We knew that when she flopped her large ears, she too was chasing off the mosquitos. We idled the motor and slipped within twenty-five feet of her. She continued to eat, watching us without concern, until finally she sauntered off. As she tried to get up on the riverbank she slipped backwards two or three times before she got a foothold and disappeared into the tangle of shrubbery.

We continued toward Coffee Creek. With so many changes in the contour of the river, I kept struggling to find the old places as they were in 1941. The large home where Phyllis and I had visited the Malloys seemed to be completely gone. I remembered them telling us how many times the river had flooded them out of their home and they always rebuilt.

We nosed up on the beach and tied the bowline to a clump of shrubs. With boots on—or wet sneakers, as mine always were—we tramped over a path that was made by an all-terrain vehicle. Coming across three-wheeler tracks was a surprise to me. My friends and I had ATVs at home, but I hadn't expected to see signs of them out here.

The wild roses were already red with rosehips, and the wild delphiniums were three or four feet tall. We had seen larkspur on the trip, but the ones here had unusually thick stocks. Had Mrs. Malloy planted the first seeds many years ago? To our disappointment the owners of a nearby cabin were not at home, and we walked around the open field and stretched our legs while we swatted mosquitos. One old log cabin seemed to have settled right down into the earth, though it appeared to be in use. There were fresh ATV tracks and supplies had been brought in. We guessed that they were prospecting, but we later learned that the owner, Cowboy Smith, was training for the Iditarod dog sled race.

It was always a relief to get back on the river and quickly away from shore and those infernal mosquitos, swarming black clouds of them! In 1941 the frost on our first night at the end of Lake Laberge must have been a blessing. If I "do the river" again, I'll take the cold in preference to warm weather. Without actually experiencing it, no one can know how close these tiny creatures can come to driving a person mad.

There were constant changes in the shoreline. We traveled quickly through a variety of trees and shrubbery and birdlife. It was late July, and the river was moving high and fast from heavy rains at the headwaters of the tributaries. Swirls of muddy water ate away at the riverbanks. Changes everywhere. The river had taken away some of the flat land that showed in our earlier pictures. There was also substantial dredging and prospecting going on, which probably contributed to the erosion. With gold prices as high as $400 an ounce, there was increased mining activity in the area.

We often had lunch breaks in mid-river, and of course we managed to be eating most of the time. There was no opportunity to lose weight. Bags of "gorp," dried fruit, crackers and cheese all taste good out there.

We stopped at Kirkman Creek and learned that the Malloys had lived there for awhile after the river forced them out of Coffee Creek. Now a young family lived at Kirkman Creek, their property landscaped with vegetable and flower gardens and a well-manicured lawn. Their house was built from part of the house where Phyllis and I had stayed with Ma and Pa Britton. The river had consumed the horse pasture and a shed or two, but the house was safe for now.

The next stop was Stewart, a settlement named after the river that enters the Yukon there. Transportation to Mayo, Yukon Territory, was via the Stewart River, but now a highway serves that area. Stewart is on a nice flat area about twenty feet up the riverbank. There were ladders leaning against the bank, so we all climbed up and were pleased to see a well-kept lawn with lots of vegetables and flowers. A family was out in their lawn chairs enjoying the pleasant sunshine and mid-afternoon breeze that kept the mosquitos away. One of the young women remembered a story her mother had told her about two young women, Mary and Phyllis, and their "little white boat," traveling down the Yukon before she was born!

We bought treats at the store and rented a cabin for the night. It was a neat log cabin with a wood cookstove. The water pump was outside beside a big stump which served as a work table. The outhouse was down a short trail and was well supplied with matches and the ever-necessary mosquito coils. Of course that invention came a long time after our first Yukon run. Next I visited the museum. Someone with some foresight had started the museum with an impressive collection of Yukon memorabilia. Some of our party went up a small river to fish, but no luck.

The Yukon must have been a mile wide at Stewart, wrapping its way around dozens of islands. We were told that the river takes out as much as twenty feet of bank every year and the residents just keep moving back. The family we visited with had moved three times. Next time, they told us, "the river can have it all!"

River steamer and Scookum—two great "ships" during their hey day in 1941.

14

The Klondike

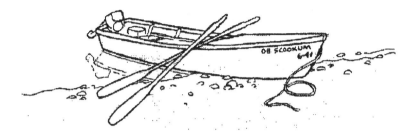

Twenty-five miles farther on we came to Ogilvie, the site of one of the first trading posts in the country. The evening was grand, and we became so engrossed with the sunset—no one can paint like Mother Nature—that we decided to shove on. The colors changed from pale yellow to golden, mingled with flaming reds and bronzes, and merged into the purple-blue of night before either of us realized it. We pulled on our sweaters to keep warm and drifted idly with the current, making headway without using the oars. The moon came out, and the river channels were plainly visible. We had no trouble following our course, until the nocturnal orb dipped behind the high mountains and we were forced to make camp on the closest riverbank.

What a night that turned out to be! We found, even before we were settled, that we'd chosen to camp on a hillside. We started a fire, and everything was so dry that before we knew it, flames were racing pell-mell up the slope behind us! We fought the fire like mad for an hour or more, until we finally thought we had it under control. Then we prepared a midnight lunch and climbed into our sleeping bags. We were nicely braced to keep from sliding down the slope, and tired enough to sleep like the dead; but no sooner were we ready to drift off to dreamland than the flames broke out again!

That finished our hope of a night's rest. We spent the rest of the night fighting that stubborn fire. The northern lights flashed on, like a gigantic neon sign in the sky. For a few moments they formed a perfect question mark above our heads. How apropos! There we were, camped on a lonely riverbank miles from nowhere, fighting a fire that simply didn't know when to quit. We were indeed asking ourselves what was going to happen next. Amazingly, we found time to laugh. It was the first campfire we'd started that we hadn't had to put another log on.

Morning dawned at last, and were we ever a sight! Our faces were blackened with smoke, our freshly washed hair tangled with leaves and brush, our overalls torn and dirty. We needed no persuasion to get under way, but we hadn't gone far when we found ourselves completely lost. Channels fanned out in every direction; which one were we to take? Our map was nowhere to be found; we didn't know what day of the week it was; and in the battle with the flames the night before, we'd forgotten to wind our one and only watch. We didn't even know what time it was!

But we selected a channel and kept on rowing, plying the oars with a vengeance. How long we rowed, I don't know. But we had chosen our channel well, for around a bend in the river the deserted buildings of Klondike City crept into view. Klondike City, more familiarly known as Lousetown, was located on a crescent-shaped flat at the confluence of the Klondike and Yukon rivers. In the early days, a fine railroad bridge had spanned the Klondike River between Dawson and Klondike City. Floodwaters had long since swept the bridge away, and all that remained of it now was a couple of old piers. Whereas in the halcyon days of the gold rush this suburb of Dawson boasted dozens of hotels, several dance halls, and a population of thousands, it was now a deserted village. When Phyl and I were through, only Joe Gatt—the brewmaster when Klondike City had a first-class brewery and bottling works—and two or three other old-timers still lived there. Joe Gatt was popularly known as the Mayor, and a character he was!

At Klondike we stopped to don our last clean slacks and "pretty up" a little before making our debut in the fabulous gold metropolis, Dawson. The very sight of that famous city gave us such a thrill as we had never experienced before! We had come 460 miles from Whitehorse and had several hundred more to go to reach Circle City; but that was all forgotten when we surveyed this, the high spot of our journey.

Phyl and I went into the first restaurant we found in Dawson. Everything was so good! Coins were constantly being fed into the nickelodeon and the music was great to hear. When we finished dinner and asked for the check, we were informed that the man who was feeding the music machine had paid for our meal too! This generous fellow turned out to be Kel Harris, a local. He told the waitress that if we would be downstairs the next morning he would take us up to the "summit," the site of the Klondike and Dawson gold diggings.

That evening we visited the waitress in her apartment, where she showed us her impressive tips—a row of gold nuggets along her window sill!

The following day Kel gave us a ride out to Hunker Summit. The various creeks, including the fabulous old Bonanza, fanned out from Dawson in every direction. Good roads branched out to the mineral regions, where gold dredges had replaced the old hand operations of the past. Kel talked about Dawson's fruitful days. In 1898 and 1899, fifty thousand people populated the town and hinterland. The population now was only a fraction of that, but the old buildings were still there to reflect the glory of a romantic past. From the tales we were told, the money really rolled in those days!

From Hunker Summit we seemed to be on a level with the surrounding mountains, whose lofty peaks, the first snows glittering from their majestic crests, presented a pageant of beauty beyond description. From that prominence we could see the vast expanse of country for miles in every direction.

In Dawson we made a pilgrimage up the hillside street behind the town to visit the little log cabin which had once been the home of Robert Service, the famous bard of the Yukon. During our rambles about the town we noticed that Dawson was a great place for bicycles. Everyone was riding them, from the tiniest tots to the most sedate old-timers. There were few cars—no doubt because of the fact that gasoline sold for a dollar a gallon. We spent two nights at the Regina Hotel. We had our own private bathroom with two bathtubs! There were also electric lights. Dawson had the first of these we'd seen since leaving Whitehorse.

Our two days in Dawson were gone all too quickly. There were many sights to see and many tales to hear of the early days, but our time was far too short to take them all in. We wanted to stay much longer, but the season was advancing, and if we were to reach our goal before freeze-up, it was imperative that we move on. Nowhere did we find people so hospitable to a couple of cheechakos as were the people in this famous city of gold. They made us feel as if we'd known them all our lives, and that no favor was too small or too large for them to do for us. Half the town showed up to wave us off on our journey.

My camp set up at the river park—the kayak is still a little unstable as the floatation tubes were not inflated and Barb hadn't adjusted the ribs.

15

Dawson Revisited

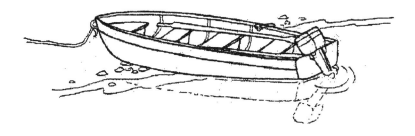

The five of us arrived in Dawson on a Sunday afternoon during a music festival. There were crowds of people everywhere. It was hot and dusty, lots of water-skiers and swimmers. The clerks and business people uptown were dressed in costumes relating to the gold rush days, and tourism was in full swing. Our arrival went unnoticed, as nowadays there are so many river travelers.

Dawson spreads in every direction. The flat terrain at the base of the mountains is a natural place for a city. There is still enough gold and other minerals in the region to give financial profit to many. Tourism also brings money to Dawson; many of the tourists we saw seemed more interested in spending money in the casinos than in enjoying the natural beauties of the Yukon.

While the city hustled, we had a job to do. We had to find the car and trailer that had been left there for us, get hotel rooms, and dismantle and pack the kayak and all our gear. We were busy. I was quite apprehensive as I helped with the kayak. I wondered how I would do on my own with the kayak that Phyllis and I were to use. It had been carried up in the car by friends. My four companions were to tow the power skiff back to Haines and onto a ferry to Juneau. We celebrated with dinner and all the trimmings at a great restaurant. The windows had red velvet drapes, heavy and ornate. We drank champagne. We had been on the water only a week, but we felt we owed ourselves a big treat.

After a couple days of sightseeing, shopping and laundry, Paul took me and my gear to a camping park on the opposite side of the river. A small ferry crosses every half hour twenty-four hours a day. We found a good camp spot, and I left all my gear in a pile beside a picnic table. We then drove back to town for a farewell breakfast and a group picture.

After my friends headed back toward Alaska, I ferried across to the campground. A few sprinkles of rain started and I tried to think what I should do first. So many thoughts running through my mind. I was alone on the shores of the Yukon! I rather wanted to sit and just watch the river roll by but I didn't dare. There was too much to do! I put the tent up first, but the rain never really materialized. The setting was perfect, with the road on one side, and the sloping bank to the river on the other. We would be able to launch our kayak easily from there—that is, if I could assemble the thing. There were nice trees for shade and privacy and lots of firewood.

I decided to start on the kayak before I lost all confidence in my ability to put it together. I dumped out the contents of the two big bags. All those peculiar pieces should go together to make a safe boat for two people. Wow, was I confused! I kept telling myself to keep calm; after all, it was my idea to do this. All the little pieces with red marks went into one pile at one end of the boat-to-be. The green ones went in a pile at the other end. So far, so good. I was starting to get excited about the challenge. Everything was going together quite well until I realized for sure that two long rods were missing. I searched and searched, but there was still a section of about four feet that needed one more pole on each side. One of the ribs didn't seem quite right, but I couldn't decide where I had gone wrong. Someone I know would have said to me, "Well, where you made your first mistake was thinking you could do it after seeing it done only once before."

There was another tent close by but nobody was moving around yet, and it was almost noon. I did wish they would wake up and perhaps help me. When they finally did, I could hear bits of their conversation and it was a foreign language. Oh, how I prayed that they'd be Germans—my kayak was designed in Germany!

I was stumped. Finally, I decided to tear some washcloths in half and wrap the ends of the rods where the missing pieces should have been. I had brought several washcloths along to use as towels and then discard them. My plan was to protect the kayak's tough outer skin from being punctured so there would be no damage. Nothing was going to stop me from continuing that trip. I was so glad that my "upriver" companions had gone back to Juneau; they would never have allowed me to continue. I was convinced, though, that the kayak was still safe. With this decision made I took time for coffee and a cup of instant soup. I built a small hot fire and was soon relaxing again and thinking, This too shall pass.

About then my neighbors, three of them, came over and asked if I had a problem. Wow, did I! I showed them the problem and with hardly a second thought one of the men said, "Wait a minute, ma'am," and dashed down to the river. He came back carrying four pieces of galvanized pipe, two of which were the exact diameter of the missing rods. I could hardly believe it! I learned later that he had seen these in a pile of river debris when he beached there a few days earlier. I was surprised to hear them all cuss in English when they saw that the pipes were too long. Before this, all their conversation with each other had been in German. I had experienced this before in the South Pacific. Are we the only people that cuss?

We could see that by cutting about six inches off of each pipe, they would snap into place exactly like the originals. This could only happen on the Yukon! We measured them carefully and I scratched the mark with a sharp rock and ran to catch the ferry so I could get them cut at a shop in town.

I caught the three o'clock ferry and carried the pipes to the city workshop. The workers there very graciously put each pipe in a vice and cut off the few inches. I can still see the astonished looks of the ferry crew when I carried those pipes aboard again. One remarked, "You didn't stay in town long!" I didn't try to explain anything; even I know that words cannot fully explain a situation. They knew I was planning a kayak trip. Did they think this old city girl thought she would need plumbing parts down the Yukon?!

Back in camp I took my fingernail file and smoothed down the rough burrs on the pipe ends. No danger now of puncturing the skin of the kayak. The pipes fit perfectly! The final step was to put each end of the framework into the skin and together they should go; and they did! I blew up the flotation tubes and it looked quite good. One of the ribs still didn't fit just right, but I couldn't see where I made a mistake, so I considered it finished.

On the first night alone in my new camp, I collapsed into bed at eight o'clock and slept for twelve hours! Much to my surprise, I may have slept longer if I hadn't had neighbors. Have you ever heard a campground waking up?

There was one familiar face at the campground, a German man we had met earlier on the trip. (It seems like the Yukon Territory and its famous river get a lot of publicity in Germany.) He was taking a strenuous three-month trip, canoeing the rivers of the region. He planned to canoe up the Porcupine River, which had long been a dream of mine.

The only reason I recognized this young fellow as he walked by in the Dawson campground was that I had seen his blue wash basin before. It had really caught my eye at the time, it was such a convenient article for a camping trip. Empty, it folded into a flat twelve-inch square, and as it filled, the sides raised. It could be used for everything! The two of us had a good visit and a cup of coffee with lots of river talk, and a good laugh over the blue basin introduction.

For two days I spent quite a bit of time in Dawson. I was disappointed to learn that people I inquired about had passed away. I constantly had to remind myself that when I was twenty years old, most of the people on the river were much older than I. Now, four decades later, it was too late in many cases to look some of the folks up. I was very upset to learn later that Mrs. Malloy had passed away while I was in Dawson, and I had lost two precious days trying to locate her.

Once when I returned to my campsite after returning a book to some newfound camp friends, there was a couple who had pulled their kayak up on the beach and were waiting for me. It turned out to be John and Barb, whom I had last seen in Glacier Bay. They figured out I must be there because they saw my quilted wallet lying on a picnic table. They knew that I would be the only one who would leave a wallet lying around! What a joyous reunion it was! Of course we had a lot of experiences to share and plots to plan for the rest of our river trips. There must be some sort of bond between those who truly enjoy the outdoors. I have often encountered such surprises.

Phyllis calls hello as she arrives in Dawson, 1983.

Standing beside the river boat Keno and feeling proud that we are the ones still running the river.

16

Reunion

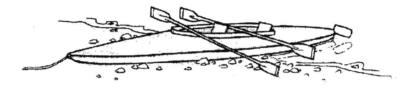

Phyllis arrived in Dawson the evening of July 28, 1983. I was a little nervous as we crossed the river on the ferry and walked to our camp. Would we both have changed a lot, and would she approve of my kayak and camping setup? And now, at our ages, could we really do what we had done when we were so much younger?

It didn't take long for it to feel like old times. We talked until midnight, still able to laugh and giggle over the foolish predicaments we'd been in. Even at midnight it wasn't really dark, and John and Barb came over, anxious to meet Phyllis. We enjoyed fresh tomatoes that Phyllis had picked from her garden that morning in California!

Phyllis had gone back to Redding, California, in 1945, after she quit working on the Alaska Railroad. Although she loved her adventures in Alaska, her friends and family were back in Susanville, near Redding, and she couldn't stay away forever.

Phyl wrote to tell me that she had a job cooking—boy, we were good cooks!—at a nightclub. She seemed happy and we kept in touch from time to time. In 1947 she met Jerald Kingsbury, a bartender at the club where she worked. Phyl probably had an inkling that this was the man for her, but she was patient and in 1948 they were married in Reno. Reno was close and exciting and lots of couples eloped to the bright lights and glitz for a quick honeymoon. Phyl was twenty-seven years old when she got married, and she was ready to start a family. Her first son, Jerry, was born soon, and within a few more years Chuck was born. Pam, her first and only daughter, came next and the last child, Danny, was born in 1955.

Times were pretty good during the post-war years. Many of the women who had spent the war years at work making war-related products had now gone back to caring for the children and maintaining the house. Having a family and a home and a husband were important to Phyl, and she soon had her hands full of the American dream.

Jerald, who was better known as "Tink," worked in timber harvest for many years, and within about ten years they were able to buy a nice home, the same home they reside in today. Phyllis worked off and on—cooking, of course—at the school cafeteria when the kids were older. But the central theme in her life was family. Phyl's life resembled a Norman

Rockwell painting—a warm, close family, where parents sat through dozens of Christmas pageants and class plays, watched the boys in all their sports, and attended many games and music concerts. Phyl passed through the rituals of motherhood, sweetening nasty-tasting cough syrup, reading thermometers, and lying awake nights while the chicken pox, mumps and measles descended on her children. Tink was often out for a week or so at a time when working in the woods, so Phyl got both night and day watch then.

They spent winter vacations skiing and summer vacations boating and fishing in the local mountain lakes and streams. The boys and their father eventually took to hunting weekends together. Phyl had a full and productive garden, and still boasts the best tomatoes and gladiolas around! Northern California was quiet and remote, even more so than today. It was a secure and wonderful place to raise a family. It was sunny and dry, and while life was not one big adventure there, it was peaceful and full of the joyful experiences that come to a family who shares every moment. Today, three of Phyl's children still live in Burney and one lives a short distance away in Redding. Most of the grandkids are within minutes from Grandma Phyl and Grandpa Tink's place.

When Phyl told her husband and kids that she was going to Alaska to run the Yukon River again, they struggled hard not to persuade her otherwise. "The kids thought a cruise would be more my style," Phyl told me. "Especially since I had never been in a kayak before!" But all in all they supported her plans. Just about the time she was ready to leave for Dawson, her son Chuck went to see her. "He thought it might be the last time he would see me alive!"

Phyl knew I had had some exciting times since we'd last seen each other. "But I also knew that I was one lucky girl to have married Tink and raised such special children as I did," she told me. "It was a soothing thought to know that my husband of forty years was patiently awaiting my return from the Yukon. It somehow made me feel safe."

Phyl and I spent a day sightseeing in Dawson. I can't count how many times we both asked, "Remember when . . .?" We walked up the hill to Robert Service's cabin. He lived there while doing some of his famous writings. We sat on the lawn with about fifty other tourists and listened while some of his verses were recited. Again, changes. In 1941 we were the only ones on the property the day we visited, and—no longer allowed today—we were able to roam inside the building and enjoy his scribbled notes on the walls. My favorite was "Goodbye Little Cabin," and I often recite it when I leave my little home in Gustavus.

We found the riverboat "Keno," but she was permanently dry-docked in Dawson. She is a museum attraction now, but we didn't go aboard the ship. Instead we reminisced about the time we had been served tea so long ago. The ship was all restored with fresh paint and looked good. Phyl and I wondered what a little fresh paint would do for us! As I took a picture of Phyllis in front of it I wanted to say, "Keno, you're not the only ol' gal who has lasted this long. At least we're still afloat on the Yukon!" And Phyllis certainly had the biggest smile.

Camping in the Dawson area held a much-appreciated surprise. The city had sprayed the entire area to discourage the mosquitos in the spring and again at regular intervals. Such a wonderful civic project! Both of us were taking vitamin C and B complex, which also seemed to help keep the mosquitos away. During the trip with my four companions on the upper part of the river, I had been annoyed by the skeeters buzzing and got bitten some, but the itch never lasted long and there was no swelling or infection. I definitely gave the vitamins credit. My companions suffered so much more.

At the campground we had interesting visits with travelers and canoeists. The highway comes in here, so there were lots of motor homes, all sizes. Two men stopped by and were most interested in our mode of transportation. Lots of questions; many people had no idea what our trip involved. After killing time with us the two men walked away, commenting that "the women should have the dishes done by now." Later Phyl and I saw the men drive by in a 35-foot motor home that would have scared me to death! Some people were envious but thought the idea of kayaking was much too dangerous. Others just took pictures and were intrigued that we old gals were repeating our trip.

Finally our day had come. John and Barb had redone the kayak so the rib was now in the proper location. Barb just shook her head when she looked at all our stuff. We too wondered if we would get it all into one kayak and still have room for ourselves. Again we looked with amazement at how perfectly the two jerry-rigged pipes fit the place where the wood poles should have been. With luck like that we would get through anything!

17

Putting In

At six in the morning, anxious and a little nervous, we slid our "yacht" down the bank to the sandy river beach. We hoped to do this while our friends were still in town. Everything fit into the kayak except for one sleeping bag, which we sealed in a canvas bag and lashed to the bow. John and Barb got back in time to see us and take pictures. The conversation included more plans and hopes to meet up along the way.

We started off like pros. Phyl was barefoot and I wore my wet tennis shoes, as usual. With spray skirts on, we were warm inside the kayak. We could still laugh but could not seem to paddle in a straight line. I had left the rudder off thinking it would do okay without it. Someone had advised us against using a rudder while others were adamant about its necessity. Since I had borrowed the kayak, I was worried about hitting bottom and damaging the rudder. By the end of that day, however, we were ready to use it.

We took a "pit-stop" mid-morning on the left side of the river; for some reason we could only travel on the left side. In the afternoon we started looking for camp spots. When we finally spotted one, we had no success fighting the current to get to it. It was something like trying to spot a motel vacancy from a busy freeway. We paddled on through heavy rain. We drifted and drank hot coffee from a thermos and told ourselves that this too would pass. That afternoon we stopped at an abandoned old trailer house and took shelter in it during a heavy downpour. We watched the muddy river roll by and commented on how different it was from our first trip when the water was clear.

We thought that we were at Ballaret Creek but our map and reference didn't jibe; but it didn't matter much to us where we were as long as we were out of the rain. When a break in the rain came we piled out and feasted on wild raspberries that were thick and well washed; no worries about insecticides there. When we got back to our kayak we found that a bear cub had left his prints there to let us know of his presence. He too had come down from the raspberry patch!

Paddling against the cold rain, we decided one day of this was enough! We soon made camp on the east side of the river. Phyl got the fire going while I put up the tent. The rain finally stopped and the hot fire dried our clothes and our spirits. We had a good clear creek and were able to wash up. We regretted that the river was so muddy. Perhaps on our first trip the river was freezing up higher so we didn't get the muddy runoff. Or was it the extensive mining that was eroding the earth?

Three seine nets were stretched across the river with a string of white floats beginning at the bank and extending out into the river. Nets were usually near an eddy in the current. Two men with a skiff and high-powered outboard motor came to tend them when the rain stopped. When they noticed our tent they started to make their way over to our side, but they evidently changed their minds when they noticed we were inside our tent. So we missed a visit there.

The rocks were an unusual color here. Of course they were wet, so they looked more spectacular. We filled our pockets rapidly, wishing we knew what we were looking at. We thought that we probably had some nephrite jade that was common in this area. And weren't some of these rocks ruby or amethyst?

We traveled about thirty miles that day, and after building a big warm fire, we were glad to crawl into our sleeping bags early. The next day was Sunday and sunshine! Such a beautiful world! We had coffee beside a big campfire and spent time just being happy that we were there. We put in the river at a lazy mid-morning hour, and with the rudder on, we made the three-mile trip to Cassiar Creek in twenty-five minutes. It was usually difficult to estimate our overall travel speed, but we thought we had definite location points here. I kept telling myself that I really must learn to operate the rudder better, but just as it had been forty-two years earlier, Phyl could still take things lightheartedly. At one point she asked me if I had really intended to go in a circle. "I wanted to see that view again anyway," she teased. Soon we put on our sweaters as the sun disappeared.

We went ashore when we spotted some people ahead in a yellow canoe. They shoved off, however, just as we reached the beach above them. We were batting zero. We had seen a working fish wheel just before Cassiar Creek but we didn't stop, not that we didn't want to, but we couldn't maneuver to it in time.

For the next two days Phyl and I paddled, drifted, and snacked on coffee, cheese and salami (made in California and eaten on the Yukon). Sometimes it was hard to find drinkable water. We never had that problem on the first trip. Such is the way of the modern world.

We got stuck on river bars a few times, and getting off of them was quite an operation. Phyl would usually get out, barefooted, and try to push me out. This didn't always work and sometimes I got out too. Getting back in was the tricky part. Phyl would get in while I steadied the boat in the knee-deep water. Then "Miss Graceful Number Two" would wobble in, and we would be off again. My arms were starting to get sore and achy but certainly not as much as I feared they would. Both Phyl and I had had our little run-ins with arthritis by now, but we amazed ourselves with our fitness.

On the first Yukon trip, we would stop any time we smelled smoke, for that meant someone was probably home. We tried to do the same on the second trip. One time I thought I smelled smoke and was readying to go ashore, when I realized that Phyl had just taken her coat out of the bow. It was our clothes that smelled of smoke!

A street in Dawson with friends who made our stay so special. One
of the few cars there in 1941.

Mary on porch of Robert Service's cabin.

18

Roll Up the Sidewalks

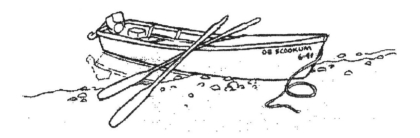

After our grand farewell in Dawson, Phyllis and I came upon the settlement of Moosehide, a tiny Athabaskan village. It sat high on a bluff, so we couldn't easily make a stop there. We kept on our way and passed by Ballaret Creek. The birds there were gathering for migration, and the autumn colors were beautiful. Forty Mile, another historic landmark of the Yukon, was our next port of call. While we were pulling up to the bank to make our usual visit and look the camp over, we were struck by the fact that the common gas can played a very important part in the life of the far north. These square five-gallon cans were vital in the various lines of human endeavor, including housekeeping.

First we saw them used as water buckets. For that matter, they were the only kind of water buckets we saw. Then, as they tarnished, they were relegated to the station of garbage cans. To make a serviceable wash boiler, the northerner would cut open one side of the gas can and roll back the edges. It was not an uncommon sight to see such an improvised boiler resting atop a Yukon stove, filled to the brim with steaming clothes. Almost always a couple of gas-can buckets of water would be heating on the back of the stove. Dog food pans, wash basins, dust pans, light reflectors, ash trays, and other smaller items were made from the gas cans. The cleverest trick, perhaps, was the way the Yukoners made stoves, even, by telescoping and soldering two cans together. Even the roofs of the houses were covered with flattened gas cans! What an extraordinarily large role, we thought, for such an apparently simple item as a tin can!

After landing at Forty Mile, we met an old-timer on the beach and asked him our exact location. "If you stop and visit awhile, I'll tell you," he returned. Of course the first thing he asked us was where we were from. When we told him California he replied, "Oh, I have a cousin there! His name is Royal Brown. Do you know him?" We couldn't help but laugh. Since there were no road signs and no city limit markings along the Yukon, any directions a cheechako could pick up were valuable, so we stopped and had a pleasant visit with the old-timer.

Back on the river, we came to the international boundary and crossed over into American territory. It gave us a good feeling to be "home" again, for in spite of the fact that we had good neighbors—no one knew better than Phyl and I just how kind and hospitable those neighbors were—still, we had been strangers in Canada. Back in Alaska, we were in the land that we belonged to, and that belonged to us.

Just before reaching the town of Eagle, we stopped to clean up. It's amazing how dirty you can get around campfires and in a boat; we certainly did! As we drew close to the town we could see a group of Athabaskans lined up on the riverbank, staring at us as if no other white girls had ever been seen on the river. We rowed past them, feeling like queer specimens of some sort under their searching eyes. Like most of the towns we passed, Eagle was located close to the bank of the river. It was the first American town we had visited since Skagway, and to us it looked pretty good, nestled picturesquely beside the broad Yukon under a sky grayed by fast-moving storm clouds.

The winter wood supply was stacked everywhere—on the riverbank, in front of the stores, and in front of the homes. To gain entrance to the general store, we had to wind our way between two huge piles of cordwood. There was a peculiar fascination in buying American brands again. Our shopping was less of a guessing game than in the Canadian stores, where we were completely unfamiliar with brands and prices. Few of the stores there had had bread in stock, so we had gotten that necessary staple from the roadhouses.

No doubt you've heard the old saw about rolling up the sidewalks at eleven o'clock each night. But in Eagle we found a new angle. The dock was actually rolled up, so to speak, each fall. Then in the spring, when the water was still high, the first section of dock was put out. As the water receded other sections were added.

In Eagle they told us that the steamer "Yukon" was stuck on a bar about a hundred miles down the river, so we were eager to get back on the water and head that way. Just as we were laughing and joking about the fun we'd have razzing the captain and crew, whom we had met before, we heard a steady chug-chug, coming upriver. Taking no chances, we rowed to the shore and waited. Soon the big river steamer came puffing around the bend, but it was under slow bell and panting upstream at reduced speed.

As it struggled up against the current and passed us, we marveled at the beauty of the big ship under the moonlight and the reflection of its lights in the water as it passed. We marveled too at the comfort and style in which the passengers on the big vessel traveled. But it gave us no remorse. So far as we were concerned, the O. B. Scookum was the ideal riverboat, and we were traveling in the most desirable way. Certainly we were learning more about the North than we could have by steaming up the river in confining luxury.

We heard later that the steamer Yukon, after we had met it, had hit another bar, and its hull was punctured so badly that a sister ship was sent from Dawson to its rescue. With the assistance of the other boat, and with pumps going steadily, the Yukon was able to continue its last voyage of the season to Whitehorse. There it was hauled onto the ways and repaired during the winter.

I believe we bought a can of Spam at this store many years ago for 50 cents. This picture was taken by one of the two prospectors who had their guns ready as we crawled up the bank and out of the brush. I believe someone repainted the sign.

19

Bear Country

We stopped at what we thought might be Forty Mile. I stumbled barefoot over the rocks to tie the kayak to a shrub. When I turned around Phyllis was passing our tennis shoes ashore on the blade of a paddle. After putting on our shoes, we headed up the bank toward some cabins we had seen from the river. There was no trail, so we crawled through the bushes, and when we came out at the top of the bank, we certainly had a surprise waiting. Two men were pointing their rifles directly at us!

They had heard us crawling through the brush but hadn't seen us. It must have been one of those rare times when Phyl and I weren't talking. Boy, were we all surprised to see each other! The men were headed to Eagle to spend the winter. Trapping? Prospecting? The four of us talked "river" for a few minutes and learned that they were the ones in the yellow canoe we had seen on the river.

Phyl and I inspected the old log buildings which had been in good condition many years before. Like so many other buildings they had probably been built farther back from the river, but with the current constantly nibbling the shore away they were now close to the bank. This all made it hard to recognize the areas that we were revisiting. In a large old two-story log building, we found a lot of cracked and dry harnesses and a rusty oil-barrel wood stove similar to the one I heat my home with. There were old iron bed frames and a grinding wheel. All were left from the busy days of mining at Forty Mile. All these heavy, large items must have been brought in by the sternwheelers coming up the river many years ago.

We found lots of wild raspberries and managed to eat a few handfuls despite the pesty mosquitos. We recalled the absence of mosquitos on our first trip and wondered how so many million mosquitos could survive with so few warm-blooded creatures in the area, but somehow they did.

Leaving the raspberries to the skeeters, we finally scrambled through the brush down to the kayak. There we went through our usual ritual, removing tennis shoes, rinsing feet, and climbing in. Phyl settled in the bow seat, rinsed off her shoes and laid them across the bow to drip. I shoved out to deeper water, settled into my seat, picked up my paddle, and we were off. We coasted into the main current doing what we enjoyed most, gliding along and experiencing the shore scenery. A friend had told me that he liked to travel on a river because it was always going some place. How true.

There were lots of small islands where the Fortymile River joined the Yukon. On one of the islands we sighted the yellow canoe and crew with a cook fire burning.

In the afternoon we saw the cut that marked the United States-Canada border. We had been looking for it for quite awhile and then realized that we had to position ourselves just right and look over our left shoulder to see it. This is a fascinating thirty-foot-wide swath that was first cut, I believe, in about 1920. Phyllis and I had seen the marker before where the Taku River, near Juneau, meets the Canadian border. It is visible for many miles and continues across the mountain ridges. Crews were working on it to keep the strip clear. Now they used chain saws but I wondered if it was all handwork the first time.

On one stop we saw several grizzly bear tracks and we felt a little smug about being able to identify their prints. Grizzlies! As we sat on the sunny bank eating (again!), a rubber raft with four passengers aboard passed by, and we all waved to each other, as if thankful there were other human beings out there.

It was the first part of August when Phyl and I came upon Eagle for the second time. Upon arrival in 1941, we had had the seal removed from our small rifle by the town constable. The Canadians had sealed the gun when we entered the Yukon. I guess Americans were not allowed to carry ready weapons. We now laughed about how we had carried the blame thing all the way to Anchorage and never even fired it.

We learned from the townfolk that John and Barb had left town a few hours earlier. We were sorry we had missed them, but as all kayakers do, we'll meet again.

After talking to the too-busy park ranger and getting a little river news we enjoyed a walk through town. A good walk was almost essential when traveling in a kayak. In our old "Scookum" we could move around freely. Even though we had expected changes we were still surprised at how much Eagle had grown in forty years. It was full of many new buildings and there was even a scheduled town tour. There were gorgeous flowers and vegetable gardens, but town was hot and dusty.

The two of us had a restaurant meal of hot roast beef and pie and ice cream—we deserved the best! We even got to wash our hands and faces in hot running water! We purchased more groceries than we needed at the general store. Everyone kept telling us, "Last store for 178 miles!" so the idea of running out scared us and we loaded up.

The river current called us and after filling our water jug, we were off again! Almost as quickly as we settled down to paddle, we were grounded! We had been paying attention to the ripples so we could gauge the depth, but sometimes the current fooled us. In places, the water rushed over big boulders and deep holes on the river bottom, creating a mass of boils on the surface. At such times it was easy to imagine scary creatures of the deep. "They're going to get us!" I often shouted as we paddled away from the waves with all our strength. Some of the back eddies were hard to get out of, and to paddle directly across the river was impossible for us. We didn't remember these problems with the O. B. Scookum. Did the difference lie with the boat, the current, or the added years of the boatmasters?

We passed a fish wheel where several men were unloading salmon, but with our boat control problems we hesitated to get too close and perhaps foul up their operation. Later we learned that they were doing a "spaghetti" count of the fish, so called because of the plastic strings used to tag the salmon.

The current caught us just right and we found ourselves against a nice sandy beach with an easy step-off. We had never landed as easily, so, feeling that we should use the beach for something, we left our boat in a foot of water and went ashore to use nature's one stop outhouse; very convenient!

We had set our watches back two hours to Pacific time, and that evening our bodies and our clocks were both confused. It may have been eight o'clock officially, but it was ten at night our time. We snacked, put up our tent, and crawled in. I awoke the next morning at five (seven, our time). I never did understand time zones, but we made it to the river by nine o'clock that morning, real time. Clouds threatened rain on and off, and there were strong headwinds. We wished we could turn our paddles to better feather the wind, but they were swollen at the joints and wouldn't budge. (Whose joints were stiff and swollen?!)

We were thrilled when on our right a black bear came down to the beach with three cuddly cubs following her. We were downwind of them and able to watch for several minutes. The cubs tumbled around, even boxed each other just like kids at play. Perfect teddy bears! Momma bear sat on her haunches and seemed to study us drifting about a hundred feet from her. The cubs washed their faces and scratched their ears, and then scampered suddenly up the bank and into the brush as if mom had commanded them to "scoot!" Mom loped right behind.

We passed Nation Creek and saw smoke on the beach near the Rock of Ages. The Rock makes for a real gusher; the water rushes over its surface, making it look like an underwater creature. It was much more of a challenge than either Five Fingers or Rink Rapids, and I was perhaps the most frightened I had ever been on the river. Before we cleared it I kept thinking about what would happen if we tripped our rudder on it. If we did I was sure we would broach and roll over. Well, we made it, of course, or I wouldn't be writing this. We must have been quite a picture, our heads down and paddles bent to get away from that rock.

Because it was our intent in the first place, we pulled up on the beach to investigate the smoke we had seen. Three of the campers asked us how many times we had rolled over! Is this the first thing that people think about kayaks?! These campers had a powerful jet boat and only two days to spend on the river.

Later, sitting low in the water and quietly paddling or drifting in our kayak, we felt good knowing that we were experiencing the river in the best possible way.

Mary with bulky kapok sleeping bags at cabin where we spent the night. Any roof was better than our tarp!

20

The Lure of the North

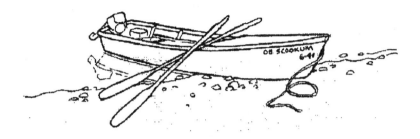

We snuggled into our sleeping bags and drifted all night. On the following day, we were in a quandary. Our detailed map had made it fairly easy to judge our position as far as Eagle. But from that point on, the map showed only the main tributary streams and islands. Where were we? On the Yukon, yes; but that's a fairly general statement. About that time we ran into some severe dust and sand storms. Phyl, with her usual subtle humor, remarked dryly, "Well, as long as we encounter dust storms, we can feel fairly certain that the ground isn't frozen yet."

That afternoon we saw a large home on the riverbank and lost no time in stopping to inquire about our whereabouts. We were surprised to learn that we had drifted and rowed eighty-five miles downstream from Eagle. Ordinarily we thought it pretty good time if we made fifty miles in a day. A young couple with two small children lived in the house, having settled there for a winter of trapping. We had dinner with them and spent the night in a small cabin on their place. As usual, we asked a lot of questions. They told us a great deal about trapping and furs, and made us envy their free, exciting, happy lives.

As our long journey was fast nearing its end, we were assailed by a flood of regrets. We felt like going on this way forever! Why go back to the humdrum ways of civilization when the lure of the North held us so firmly? We longed to roam the hills and valleys, as free as the caribou that knew no other way.

But jobs were waiting for us in Anchorage, and we knew well enough that our lust for adventure would never be thoroughly satiated. As we stopped to make camp or cook lunch and boil tea, we planned and plotted other trips we'd like to make. Then it would start to rain or snow, and our plans would go scattering to the four winds while we hustled to break camp, pack our boat, wrap up in our extra clothes and go drifting down the great, winding river.

As we progressed, we came across numerous hunters going out after caribou. Evidently fresh meat was scarce at both Circle and Fort Yukon, for the hunters were eager to know whether we'd seen signs of game along our way. All we had seen were tracks.

That afternoon we really hit a cloudburst! We were nearing the Arctic Circle, and the weather was growing colder all the time. The rain drenched us, and we were so cold and miserable that we stopped at an old-timer's cabin to warm up. He pleaded with us to stay overnight. When we told him we had hopes of reaching Circle City that night, he laughed and drawled, "Well, what you can't do today, you can always do tomorrow." That simple sentence truly summed up the philosophy of the North country; we met it time after time. No hurry, no rush. Take things easy and worry not. So spoke the contented citizens of that wide, free land, truly the land of day after tomorrow, or year after next. Time marched on, yet stood still. But in its wake it left a carefree, happy people, thankful for their lot and for the radiant goodfellowship of their far-scattered neighbors.

So we stayed. He was indeed a genial host and regaled us with many dramatic stories from his past. We were fascinated, and the delight he felt in reliving his experiences for us, recalling the venturesome days of his youth, made our pleasure in sharing those experiences with him even more keen. He told us of trapping ventures, how he traveled his trap lines back and forth every day by dog team, always wondering what luck the next trap would bring. The trapping game sounded as exciting to us as the quest for gold. He told us stories of the river and the mountains, stories about the wild animals, stories of the northland that only a true sourdough could tell.

Through clouds of fragrant tobacco smoke he waxed sentimental, but he meant every word he said. "Here I am, an old man. But I have had much real happiness. The caribou cross the river in front of my cabin door. The fish swim by in the river. My garden gives me plenty of vegetables. These mountains are alive with fur and game. Why, I've a fortune in my front yard. And there's nobody here to yell at me or to make me rush. What more could a man ask for?"

Late in the evening, the old sourdough said it was time to retire. Phyl and I looked at each other and then over at the one bunk in the corner. We were both thinking that perhaps we'd been a little hasty agreeing to spend the night at the old man's place. He lit a lantern and told us he was "going for a walk."

He returned after awhile and informed us again that it was time for bed. He had us follow him outside and down a long path to a cozy log cabin! That old sourdough enjoyed company so much that he had built a special cabin near his own for guests to use. He had built a fire and carried our sleeping bags up from the boat. They were spread neatly on the big wooden frame bed. A kerosene lamp was burning on the table. It was almost luxurious, and Phyl and I lay awake a long time talking about our good fortune in meeting these river folks. It seemed that each visit was more interesting than the last, and we dreaded having the trip end. But it must.

In the morning, our host crept in and built a fire. Later he returned with mugs of strong, hot coffee. I believe it was the caffeine that kept those old-timers going. Later, after a hearty breakfast of sourdough hot cakes, toast and oatmeal "mush"—we ate it all!—we thanked the old man for his kindness and shoved off on the last thirty miles of our never-to-be-forgotten journey.

Phyl and I thought about the old man often after that. He knew that some day he would reach the end of the trail, that he would have to face that last adventure alone, as he had the others. But he didn't care. Many a sourdough of the far north had been injured and had frozen to death on the trap line; fallen through the ice and drowned; killed by a surly bear; or taken ill and died in his bed before help came. But somehow we knew, after talking to this old sourdough, that he knew all that, and that wherever the trail opened out into the great beyond, he would mush on patiently, with no anguish nor regrets. To him life had already paid, in bountiful measure, for the sacrifice it demanded at the end.

Between us and Circle lay the Yukon Flats. Along that stretch the river widens until it looks like a sea, and false channels stretch out to entice the unwary. If you take the wrong channel, you might drift for days before getting back into the main current! We had been warned again and again about the Flats and were doubly careful not to get into them on a bad start. Fortunately, we hit the right course and made good time. One last high bluff loomed ahead. We rowed around it and there, directly ahead, was the town of Circle. Circle, back in the heyday of the gold boom, had been the largest log-cabin city in the world. Many of the old buildings still remained.

We had been five weeks on the river and were simply bursting with the thrills and adventures we had encountered. There had been hardships, true, and struggles enough to temper our enthusiasm. But it had all been fun. We looked upon the mighty Yukon as a symbol, almost a personality; it had taken on a human quality and we felt a lasting attachment. Our glorious adventure was now in the past, but it had been all we had hoped for.

It was a sad time when we sold our faithful O. B. Scookum, the little skiff that had been our home through so many hectic, thrill-packed days and nights. A lump rose in our throats as we turned our backs to the river and headed over the Steese Highway to Fairbanks. There we caught the train for Anchorage, and the end of our trail—this time. But we knew there would be other northern trails that Phyl and I would follow together. Already we were looking ahead, dreaming about the next adventure and where it would lead. For the lure of the North was in our blood, and it could not be resisted for long.

Calico Bluff is a popular landmark (river mark) that can be seen for quite a distance. The current takes a boat right up to the base of it.

The sign tells it all. Perhaps it could be said that this was the only road sign we saw on the Yukon River. It was the end of the trip in 1941 and again in 1983.

Phyllis and the kayak. We had chosen a bad spot to go ashore to reach a creek entering near here.

Phyllis dismantling the kayak and debating whether to discard the two galvanized pipes that had made it possible to continue the trip after my friends had driven back toward the ferry and Juneau.

We tried to imagine spending a winter here. With a lot of good books, plenty of food and knitting it might be fun?? And the river would be frozen, so perhaps friends with dog teams would visit us.

In the evening Phyllis walked along the bank for one last long look at the river that had been our host for two memorable trips.

21

End Again

The last days on the river we drifted past Calico Bluffs, which was perhaps the most interesting sight on the river. Stratified in this unusual rock formation were color patterns that almost rippled. A bend in the river made a huge cut into the folds of the colored rock. I hoped my pictures were good.

At Miller's Camp we found a log cabin with a sod roof, so old that the house had settled a few feet into the ground. It was in poor condition but had been recently used by a very ingenious person. There was a sawhorse made from a natural stump with legs in all the correct places. A boat hook had been made from a ten- or twelve-foot-long branch with its own natural limb forming the hook. Young fruit trees had recently been planted. Phyllis and I were always sorry when we missed a visit with such a resident.

As we neared the Yukon Flats, we continued to be fooled by the currents as we tried to decide which side was best to take around an island. We would check the ripples and make our decision before it got too late, but often the wide areas we chose had sandbars and shallow water.

A variety of waterfowl congregated wherever a clear creek came into the main river. Eagles also gathered around the clean streams. We weren't the only ones dismayed by the muddy water.

Phyl and I looked for familiar sights near Coal Creek. Soon we saw a road, and there were canoes on the beach. We were anxious for talk so we paddled in. Shore landings can be quite an operation. We headed for what we thought was a smooth beach and ended up in some horrible mud that was so black that we knew it had to be Coal Creek. What a mess we were in, like being mired in a barnyard. One of the canoeists invited us to the shelter for tea and talk. The shelter was the Slavin Creek park building, and though the rangers were out on patrol they had left a welcoming note so that we could enjoy the comforts and a good visit.

As usual we had to search awhile for drinking water but we finally found a good spot and set up camp. There were moose and wolf tracks everywhere! No use to worry about that now. We got a big fire going, set up the tent—this always seems to make a beach look like home to me—and cooked a hot meal.

The last morning on the river we awoke to the fascinating patterns of the steam rising off the calm waters. I also awoke to a flat air mattress. The only air left was in the pillow section. It had been a restless night for me; I woke up at four in the morning when it poured rain. But coffee, real coffee this morning, seemed to help. That decaffeinated stuff the day before just didn't cut it. We had been sore and stiff all day, and we were convinced that it was because we missed the "leaded" stuff.

That day we kept imagining all sorts of objects along the banks. I suppose we were excited about reaching our destination, and we kept expecting to see Circle just around the next bend. A big black thing was materializing ahead. "A big barge ahead!" "Yeah, and there's a man standing on it fishing." As we got closer, the "man" became two women and they were waist deep in the river trying to free a large raft from a sandbar. We offered to help but they assured us that all was well. Soon they were free and using two large sweepers to steer with.

Soon we saw an attractive cabin with a greenhouse, flowers and lawn over on the right side of the river. We decided it must be the Smith's place, people whom we had heard about and wanted to visit. But to our disappointment, by the time we saw the cabin it was too late to navigate a crossing to the bank. On we went. Circle City was about twenty miles ahead so we paddled to the left of the river. Our hopes rose as we kept watch for the last high bluff that we had found easily on our first trip.

The day was overcast with light rain and mist. No sun. An occasional bright spot broke through to give us a color show of grey and mauve. It caught our attention but we kept looking for the landmarks listed on the chart. One of these was a big island, and after some time we decided that we had the island on our right, so Circle would be coming up.

But no Circle City! We were both getting pretty concerned; maybe we had missed it! Fort Yukon was another hundred miles, a frightening prospect. Instead of admitting we were worried, Phyl pulled out her lemon drops and I snacked on peanuts. I noticed we were eating them a lot faster than usual. Several times we saw houses on the beach which turned out to be stumps. Sometimes we even thought we saw smoke coming out of them! Ridiculous what you see when you want something!

The landscape got flatter and flatter, just like the dreaded Flats we had read about. Clouds gathered above us and we started to get cold. We ate crackers and cheese and our last orange. Finally, we heard the sound of a motor and a dog barking! Town!! We reached Circle City at four in the afternoon.

We made a pretty decent landing right in front of town. When we disassembled the kayak we threw out the two make-shift pieces that had saved the day in Dawson. We rented a room with a shower; no tent tonight! The owner lent us his truck to carry our gear. He had never seen us before, but that's just the way of Alaskans!

Our reunion was over, and a world class one it was. In our twenties Phyl and I often dreamed about more great adventures in the northland, but neither of us ever imagined that we would make a Yukon re-run in our sixties. Forty-two years had not dampened the spirit that gave us such a wild notion the first time.

People have often asked Phyllis and me how two girls ever happened, in 1941, to make that long, uncertain trip from Juneau to Circle. When they ask, we rather wonder ourselves how we happened to do it. If we'd known exactly what we were getting ourselves into, maybe we wouldn't have dared. Or would we have? Yes, I guess we would have, because we were both thirsty for adventure, and probably no thoughts of danger or hardships would have given us pause.

The trip was touch and go at times, we tell people, but so it goes in a sixteen-foot skiff prayerfully named the O. B. Scookum.

ABOUT THE AUTHORS

Mary Hervin was born on a California homestead in 1921. After graduating from high school in Redding, California, she moved to the "far north." In 1939 she arrived in Juneau, Alaska, with five dollars left over to start her new life. Mary has been seeking adventures ever since. She lives a simple life in Gustavus where she enjoys kayaking, cooking, babysitting, writing and outdoor adventures. She visits with her sons— commercial fishermen—and her grandkids every chance she gets. Mary prefers the solitude of her community, which lies at the head of Glacier Bay, to the fast life.

Karen Signe Martinsen lives in Sitka, Alaska. Born in 1957 into a family of fishermen and boatbuilders, her family enjoyed many years of cruising and sailing in the San Juan Islands and British Columbia. Karen is a human resource development specialist and provides training and consulting on a state-wide basis. She has lived and traveled throughout Alaska (and seventeen foreign countries as well) and has been a commercial fisherwoman in Bristol Bay. She loves writing, photography, boating, and diving, and her life goal is to sail around the world. Her idea of adventure is "living in the gap" and letting nature take its course. Karen finds wilderness experiences essential to developing a sense of balance, wholeness and spirituality.